# LOST IN THE SHELIKOF

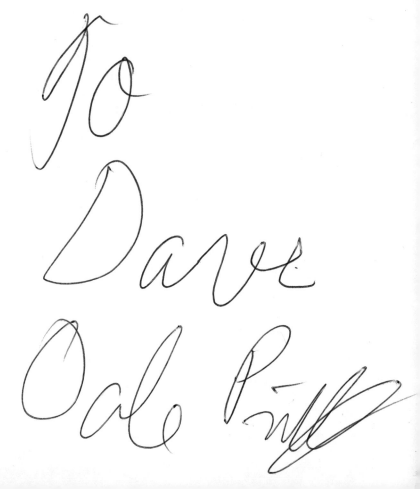

To

Dave

Dale Pr...

ISBN: 145650584X
ISBN-13: 9781456505844

### Permissions

*Sea Storm* photo reprinted with permission from the United States Coast Guard. Maps courtesy of World Sites Atlas.

Cover design by Jeff Casper Productions.

Quantity discounts are available on bulk purchases of this book for educational or gift purposes. Special books or book excerpts can also be created to fit specific needs. For information, please contact Nolan Brown Press, 44039 28th Street West, Lancaster, CA 93536; or by visiting www.lostintheshelikof.com.

# FOR TRACI AND RADELL
## -THANKS

### *Acknowledgements*

*I would like to acknowledge the good people of Kodiak for their inviting hospitality during my two visits while writing this book. The folks I met there (too many to mention individually) treated me with warmth and kindness leading me to fall in love with the place and its people. I also wish to express my gratitude to the extended Pruitt family (especially Dale, Mindy, Calista, Cally, and Mitchell) who opened their home and their hearts and made me feel like one of their own. Thanks for sharing this story with me. You are truly a special family and I'm damn glad to know you. Also, I'd like to thank my father, Bruce, who threw sand under my spinning wheels and pushed me through to the finish line. I love you. A great many thanks as well to Bobbi Carlson, my editor; your hard work on my manuscript is greatly appreciated. Finally, I'd like to thank Calvin, Natalie, and Sarah. You kids are "beast".*

# LOST IN THE SHELIKOF

## AN ALASKAN FAMILY'S STRUGGLE TO SURVIVE

# JEFF MITCHELL
## WITH
# BRUCE MITCHELL

NOLAN BROWN PRESS
LANCASTER, CA

# ALASKA

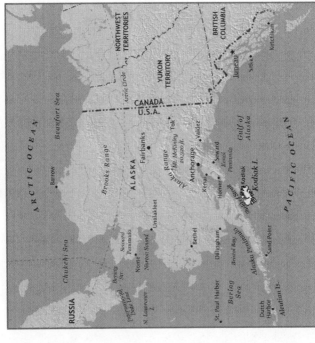

KODIAK CAN BE FOUND OFF OF THE SOUTHERN COAST OF THE ALASKAN MAINLAND. THE BODY OF WATER SEPARATING THE TWO IS THE SHELIKOF STRAIT.

# The Voyage of the F/V *Magnum*

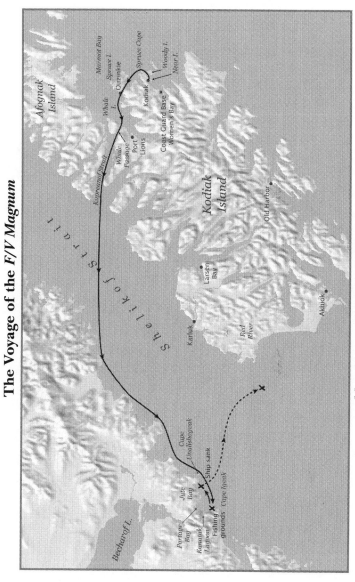

Afognak Island

Marmot Bay
Spruce Cape
Spruce I.
Ouzinkie
Woody I.
Near I.
Whale I.
Kodiak

Whale Passage
Port Lions
Coast Guard Base
Women's Bay

*Kupreanof Strait*

*Shelikof Strait*

*Kodiak Island*

Old Harbor

Larsen Bay

Kaflak

Red River

Aktiok

Cape Ubaliklugak

Ship sank

Cape Igvak

Jute Bay

Portage Bay
Kanatak Lagoon
Fishing grounds

Becharof L.

Maps courtesy of World Sites Atlas

THE PRUITT HOME TAKEN FROM PRUITT LANE.

*A wooden support beam runs along the ceiling of the Pruitt home in Kodiak, Alaska. It runs horizontally across the main room of the house. It acts as an unofficial dividing line between the family room and entry way. The beam's maroon tone offers a contrast with the white ceiling above it. In bold capital script, the word **HOME** appears. It's the first thing that catches your eye as you walk in the front door. Next to this word, in smaller cursive script, is the quote, "**Home is where your story begins**". This quote doesn't stand out as much as the boldly printed HOME does, but that does not diminish its relevance. For this story of peril and heroism; hopelessness and optimism; this story of uncertainty and conviction begins and ends here. In the Pruitt HOME – on Pruitt Lane – in Kodiak, Alaska.*

# Chapter One

M indy Pruitt sat in her silent home. Her teeth were brushed and her flannel pajamas were on. It was chilly in the house in spite of the fact that it was summer solstice. She wanted to challenge someone to a bowling match on the Wii, but she was alone. *No fun to play by myself,* she thought. So she grabbed the remote and flipped on the TV. Five fruitless minutes of channel surfing later, Mindy gave up, turned it off, and went upstairs to bed.

"Get your survival suits on!"

Calista Marie Pruitt couldn't believe what she was hearing.

"What are you talking about Dad?" She wailed, "What are you talking about? Oh my God! I didn't say *I love you* to Mom and Grandma. Dad, you can't be serious!" She was in full panic mode. Outside of their small fishing vessel the wind was blowing 50 miles per hour and the world had turned very dark indeed.

"I am serious Calista! Get your suit on! Now!"

She sprang into action. She yelled to the others resting in their cramped forward bunks. Exhausted from two full days of fishing. The fishing had not been very good.

"Mitchell, Cally......Survival suits!"

Mitchell Pruitt was already out of his bunk. Grabbing the survival suit that Calista threw his way he quickly made his way up to the wheelhouse. The boat was in a 45 degree list to the starboard side. Mitchell Pruitt, the son of skipper Dale Pruitt, was eighteen years of age. He would be leaving for college in the lower 48 after what was to be his dream summer, crewing for his hero.

And in this moment his hero was yelling to him. In his dad's voice, he could sense the danger.

"Mitchell, vang the boom!"

Following his father's orders, he quickly but carefully made his way out the door to the listing deck of the F/V *Magnum*. Levers on a hydraulic lift powered the large, steel boom from the starboard to the port side. The weight shift soon righted the vessel.

"Why don't we just go into a bay and tie up for the night?" Shrieked Cally Pruitt as she emerged from her bunk.

"I'm trying Cally. That's what I'm trying to do," He growled between tight lips, gritted teeth.

Deckhands Calista Marie and Cally Rose Pruitt struggled into their survival suits in the wheelhouse. Captain Dale had disengaged the auto pilot and manually turned the boat to the port side, toward the Alaskan mainland. She was like a sea-logged beast, sluggish and unresponsive.

The weather had changed dramatically in the hour since the crew of the *F/V Magnum* got underway for their seventeen-hour journey home to Kodiak, Alaska. The steady but moderate southwest winds battled during the previous 48 hours had violently shifted to the northwest and more than doubled in velocity.

The *F/V Magnum* was in southern Alaska, just off the upper-northeast portion of the Alaskan Peninsula. Local Kodiak fishermen call this area "big boy country". Due west, on the other side of the thin peninsula, are Bristol Bay and the Bering Sea. Brutal Arctic weather from the Bering Sea attacks the Alaskan Peninsula's western shore with full force. At 2,055 feet of elevation,

Deer Mountain and the other peaks of the Aleutian Mountain Range offer little resistance to the massive force of these relentless winds. Intense gusts of wind called williwaws scream off the eastern leeward slopes around Cape Igvak and wreak havoc on the small salmon seiners that come to these fishing grounds from Kodiak across the Shelikof Strait.

The skipper struggled with the heavy wind and the wallowing vessel. The momentary relief that switching the boom brought had waned as the boat's momentum quickly rolled back into a heavy list to the port side.

"Mitchell! Again!" Dale shouted to his son.

The first mate responded immediately. He scrambled through the door to the controls outside and sent the boom back across the stern to the starboard side. Then he ran back inside to put his emergency suit on. The neoprene survival suits are bright red. When fully donned, the only exposed portions of the body are the eyes and nose.

On the night of June 20, 2007 in the Shelikof Strait, fifteen year old Calista Pruitt was the only crew member of the *F/V Magnum* to get her survival suit completely on. Deckhands, Mitchell and Cally Pruitt only managed to get their suits partially on. Captain Dale Pruitt would lose his in the ensuing chaos. The force of the violent northwest winds rocked the vessel back into a heavy starboard list.

Survival suit on, Calista heard a crash. She swung around to see a drawer full of tools fly. Metal shot throughout the wheelhouse. She ducked down to take cover, eyes scanning the chaos. Looking over her shoulder she saw a red flashing light underneath the main captain's desk.

"Dad! What's that light?"

"What light?"

"That light. Down there. By your legs." She said pointing to a flashing red light tucked underneath a shelf near the Captain's chair. The skipper was busy fighting the seas. He briefly bent down and tried to see the alarm, but couldn't take his attention off the pitching boat.

"What's it say?"

"Laz!" She yelled.

"Oh Jesus!"

Calista knew it was bad. The harsh tone of her dad's voice telegraphed his unmistakable tension. Cally and Mitchell kept struggling with their survival suits as the hollow loud boom of each wave reverberated throughout the cabin. The relentless sea pounded their port side and was playing havoc with the Magnum's balance. Each explosion worsened their situation. A loud crash and Dale looked to his right. Water was rushing into the wheelhouse through the quickly submerging starboard window.

Cally Rose was still fighting with her suit, but with her hands in the gloves she couldn't get the zipper closed.

In a state of pure terror she screamed, "Uncle Dale!!! Help me get this on! I can't get it zipped!"

In the midst of a last ditch effort for control of the boat Dale stayed focused. His whole attention was on keeping the boat on an even keel so it was quite logical that Cally's zipper didn't take first place in this immediate universe.

"Zip it up Cally, you got to get it on. I'm sending out a mayday!" He yelled as he was knocked into the wall by another wave.

"Dad! Get your suit on!" Mitchell was screaming. "Get your survival suit on Dad," he hollered repeatedly.

Dale gave no sign that he even heard Mitchell.

"Everybody get in the skiff! Get off the boat!" He yelled again and again. A small metal skiff (small boat) was lashed to the stern of the *Magnum* for the tow back home.

Dale Pruitt's crew, his family, scrambled to the cabin door leading to the pitching deck. He picked up the receiver to the VHF radio and did the thing he'd prayed he would never have to do in his twenty-seven years as a commercial fisherman.

"Mayday, mayday, this is the *F/V Magnum* two miles off Cape Unalishagvak in distress!  Mayday!"

The cabin was rapidly filling with water.  There was no more time for idle radio chatter.  Grabbing his survival suit he made his way through the door and onto the half-submerged deck of the boat.  He saw that Calista and Mitchell were already near the skiff.

"Cally?" he bellowed.

Dale turned sharply to his left when he heard her panicked and desperate scream.  "Help!  Uncle Dale!"

He saw that his eighteen year old niece, Cally Rose Pruitt, was in the frigid, turbulent ocean.  Dark and cold, heavy winds were pushing her farther from the boat every second.  Debris spilled from the deck of the boat and surrounded her.  Dale spotted lines floating in the water near her and yelled for her to grab one.  He knew that if she drifted too far away they'd never find her.  He hoped and prayed that she could hang on until they could come get her.  He considered jumping in to save her right then, but quickly thought better of it.

Instead, he sloshed his way sternward to the skiff and jumped in with Calista and Mitchell.

When Dale Pruitt's family moved to Alaska, he had just turned twelve years old. Sid and Shirley Pruitt moved their family from Omaha, Nebraska to Kodiak in 1972.

Family friends had migrated north and talked Sid and Shirley into coming. They sold their house, bought two Dodge pickup trucks, loaded up their family of twelve, and made tracks northwest out of Omaha.

With only six interior spots in the pickups, there were always at least seven kids sharing the space under the wooden, homemade camper shells in the pickup beds. The first leg of the journey took them through Helena, Montana; then north into Canada through Calgary and Edmonton, Alberta. Inside the cramped little caravan, Pruitt's were elbow to elbow as they plodded 4,000 miles north through British Columbia, the Yukon Territory, and into Alaska. Ten days after leaving Omaha, the family arrived in Kodiak aboard the Alaskan State Ferry, *M/V Tustumena* and set foot on the remote northern island that was to become their home.

On the very next day, Sid and Shirley bought a modest three-bedroom house on Hemlock Street. They spent the first week modifying the garage into an extra room for the four older boys. The younger boys were in one bedroom while two Pruitt girls shared a room which left the parents a master bedroom. Sid and Shirley would raise their ten children in this house.

The Pruitts helped to build modern Kodiak. Sid had no carpentry experience, but he got his first job constructing the new Kodiak high school. In turn, all of his children went to the school that he helped build.

Kodiak is an archipelago and Dale helped build the Fred Zharoff Bridge connecting nearby Near Island to Kodiak Island. Today, Kodiak's big boat harbor is on Near Island. All of the Pruitt brothers have worked on construction and road projects around town and are deeply involved in the fabric of Kodiak life. This family's stamp is everywhere in this modern fishing village.

Kodiak is located at 57 degrees north latitude and 152 degrees west longitude. Located along the southern edge of central Alaska, it is the second largest island in the United States. Only The Big Island of Hawaii is larger. Thirty miles off the southern shore of the Alaskan mainland, Kodiak Island is wild and rugged wilderness. The thirty-mile wide body of water that separates Kodiak Island from the mainland is named Shelikof Strait.

The weather here is somewhat mild by Alaskan standards. But it can be treacherous as it is under the influence of major Arctic storm systems that sweep down from the north, as well as, Bering Sea storms from the west. Through the Bering Sea and over the nearby Alaskan Peninsula to the west, Kodiak is frequently hit by these arctic weather systems. But, locals are used to the wind, rain, and snow and get through tough winters by looking forward to summer days. There's nothing like a warm, sunny, summer day in a place like Kodiak, Alaska.

Dale's love affair with Kodiak began as soon as he arrived. He played   basketball for the Kodiak Bears in high school. He began crewing on fishing boats at the age of fourteen. He dreamed of becoming a commercial fisherman. Life was good and so was the fishing. He worked aboard several local boats and began to make serious money.

As a young man, Dale developed a reputation as a hardnosed, tough, reliable fisherman. He worked hard, played hard, and feared nothing. He worked winters crabbing in the Bering Sea, a very dangerous and sometimes deadly line of work.

Mindy Graham from Castle Rock, Washington was going to school at Pacific University in '82. After her freshman year, she was excited because she was going to earn good money working in a cannery for the summer in Kodiak, Alaska. Her friend, Vicky Norton, persuaded her to go to work in the Icy Cape Cannery in Kodiak where her father was plant manager. That summer Mindy met Dale. They were married on December 6th, 1983.

The new couple fished for salmon together in the waters around Kodiak aboard the *Calista Marie*. The fact that they would later christen their little girl, Calista Marie speaks volumes. This was an important time in the young lovers' lives. With the money they made they bought a cabin on Island Lake, three miles outside of the town of Kodiak. Dale had been running the *F/V Calista Marie* for the boat's owner, Louis Iani (pronounced Yanni) since '81. *Calista Marie* is a 42 foot salmon seiner. Together, Dale and Mindy built the family business, buying the boat from Louis in '85

Mindy often worked on their beautiful new seiner in the early years of their marriage. Then the family began to grow. In 1989, Mindy gave birth to Mitchell Pruitt. He was named after Mitchell Keplinger, one of Dale's best friends. Mitchell was followed three years later to the day by their daughter, Calista Marie. Both kids were born on April 6th.

*Combined with several adjacent islands, Kodiak consists of a northern land mass approximately 170 by 40 miles. The region is hilly with some mountain peaks. The highest one is 4,400 feet, much lower than the Alaskan mainland peaks to the north and east. The island is shrouded in fog for much of the year. Average annual rainfall is about 60 inches, although some parts of the island normally receive more than 90 inches.*

*The northern portion of Kodiak Island is covered with Spruce trees. Traveling from north to south, the Spruce forest gradually morphs into grasslands which are good for grazing. Cattle and sheep are raised in these areas. The coastline is deeply indented and well suited to sea travel because of a plethora of safe, natural harbors.*

# CHAPTER TWO

Dale always dreamed about his fishing business becoming a family affair. Having Mitchell and Calista on his crew could be a dress rehearsal for their taking over the business upon his retirement. The summer of 2007 was shaping up to be the fruition of that dream.

He thought about his crew. Mitchell had recently turned eighteen, a fully grown man; agile, strong, and tough. The two had always been extremely close. Mitchell and Dale split logs together for countless hours outside of their home. Young Mitchell always tried desperately to keep up with his dad at any job and when Dale was in town Mitchell was sure to be somewhere near.

Many Alaskans aren't too impressed by the celebrity heroes of the lower 48; and the Pruitts are no different. Their heroes are family and friends; the people you split wood with to keep warm in the winter; the ones ready to lend a hand in a time of need. The Pruitts are Alaskans through and through. Pure, blunt, outspoken; a close caring family.

On this trip, Dale wasn't much concerned about his son. Mitch was ready. He was to be the skiff man. The skiff man is the crewman who operates the smaller boat called a skiff. Salmon seining requires two boats: the main boat and the smaller skiff. The skiff operator attaches one end of the seine (the large net that fisherman use to catch Pacific salmon) and runs it out away from the main boat. This seine has colorful, Styrofoam floats attached to a line connecting the top edge and a heavy line called the lead along the bottom. At first glance, the lead looks like a standard nautical line. But it actually has a lead core that makes it quite heavy. When the skiff pulls the seine away from the boat, the floats keep the top edge of the net bobbing on top of the water, while the leads sink the bottom edge of the net. The result is a huge vertical trap in the water. Placing that trap in the path of a moving school of salmon is the object for the fishermen.

After pulling the net tight, it sits in the water. *Making a set* is what fishermen call this. A *set* can last for thirty minutes or so. The two or three crew members on board look forward to the short respite that comes with having the net set in the water.

Meanwhile, skippers and skiff men are busy. Artfully they maneuver their floating net with gentle throttle thrusts on each vessel. If things go as planned, the skiff man encircles the net around the unsuspecting schools of fish. Gently he creates the shape of the number 9 out of the line of floating corks. Eventually, he brings the seine full circle and the team creates a large circular net curtain in the water.

Modern skiffs are equipped with a mounted VHF radio. The Magnum's skiff had this perk. Mitchell would use the small receiver to get his instructions from Dale.

Mitchell loved working the jet-powered skiff. Jet skiffs make it easier for operators to work without fear of fouling the prop with the seine. A jet boat also frees the skiff man from worrying about grounding the propeller. Sometimes salmon run very near the shore and skiff men often have to navigate right up to the water's edge. Jet boats, having no propeller, are perfect for maneuvering near the shallow shoreline.

The skiff man plays a very important role in salmon seining. Dale's son, Mitchell was ready for the job.

Calista, he wasn't completely sure about. His daughter wasn't an average fifteen year old girl. She was strong and tough. But after all, she was still fifteen years old. While that concerned him some, Dale had a feeling that she'd be okay.

The third crew member was to be James Pruitt. James was Dale's nephew, the youngest son of his oldest brother, Sid. He had completed his junior year of high school. His family lived less than a quarter mile from Dale and Mindy. He, Mitchell, Calista, and his sister Shelby were like brothers and sisters growing up together on Island Lake. Because James was a linebacker for the Kodiak High football team and the team spent the week of June 18th 2007 at the All-Alaskan Football Camp at Colony High School near Wasilla, he had to miss this first trip of the summer on the *F/V Magnum*. But he would be back in time for the other trips and he couldn't wait to go. A summer spent fishing with Mitchell, Uncle Dale, and Calista making good money; what more could a kid from Kodiak want?

So Dale was one crewmember short for the first trip of the season. He needed to find a replacement. His first thought was of his nephew Tim, son of his brother Jeff. At age 19, Tim had fishing experience, but he had just joined the union and taken a job at his Dad's shop. He loved fishing, but couldn't get away. He suggested his sister Cally to Dale. Cally had a job at the Channel Side Chowder House. They figured that her boss wouldn't mind if she took off for a few days. Kodiak, first and foremost, is a fishing town. Fishing trumps most other occupations.

Dale called her on Father's Day, 2007.

"Cally, come fishing with me for a few days. We're going out tomorrow. James doesn't get back until later in the week. I need your help."

"I don't know Uncle Dale, I have to work."

"Well call in; I know your boss Mary Jane will let you off for a couple of days. We'll be back by Thursday at the latest to pick up James."

"I still got my cast. You think I can do it?" Cally's arm had been broken in a fall three weeks prior.

"You'll be fine. It's Calista's first trip so it'll be a real learning experience anyway. You'll be fine."

"Alright, I'm calling Mary Jane."

Two hours later Cally and her uncle were at Sutliffe's True Value Hardware buying rain gear and a commercial license.

Cally told Dale she'd be going "out the road" to see her parents first. In Kodiak, "out the road" means any of the three roads that lead out of town. It doesn't take long in Kodiak to get out of town and into the middle of nowhere.

After buying her license and fishing gear, Cally went home and threw her laundry into the machine. Then she went out the road to join the family's Father's Day celebration. When she returned home that night, she packed a bag for the trip and went to bed.

*Fishing has always been the mainstay of the economy of Kodiak Island. This demanding industry provides most of the employment for the island's residents. In addition to salmon, halibut, cod, rockfish, and herring, the island's waters have abundant quantities of crab, shrimp and scallops.*

*Kodiak Island has been described as a far-off, lonely place with limited usable shoreline regions. Indeed, the geography of Kodiak Island has restricted the number of coastal settlements. Only about 13,000 people live on the island. Most live in and around Kodiak Town, but a few thousand still live in isolated fishing villages scattered about the island. Access to these tiny burgs is limited to boats or small planes. Many villagers in Akhiok, Karluk, Larsen Bay, Old Harbor, Ouzinkie, and Port Lions still make their living the same way as the Allutiqs on the island have for centuries. Using a system called set netting, fishermen use small boats to run a net from a set point on shore out into the surf. Crews on shore then hopefully pull the nets full of beautiful Pacific Salmon onto the beach.*

*Each of the six main fishing villages has certain features in common; a small school, an Orthodox Church (a testament to the Russian influence in Alaskan State history), a landing strip, and a small harbor.*

# CHAPTER THREE

It was Monday, June 18th 2007 when skipper Dale Pruitt eased the 56 foot seiner away from the transient dock of Kodiak Harbor.  His crew coiled line while the *F/V Magnum* slowly steamed out into the narrow channel.  The *F/V Magnum* was a leased vessel.  Pruitt's own boat, *Calista Marie*, was old and tired.  She also didn't have a Refrigerated Sea Water (RSW) system.  Prior to 2005, Kodiak seiners kept their catch fresh with holds full of ice.

Now most canneries require expensive RSW systems.  Dale had run thousands of trips on the *Calista Marie*.  He had many highline years on his boat.  The new regulations presented Dale with a dilemma:  install expensive new equipment on his small boat, or buy a new vessel.  Mindy and Dale had chosen to buy a new seiner, but hadn't found one they liked. The *F/V Magnum* was available for lease. Dale chose to fish the season with it.

As usual, Mindy had been at the dock to see Dale off. But this trip was different. The new crew was her husband, her niece, her only son, and her baby, Calista. She had a mother's uneasy feelings. She had talked to Dale about her anxieties. Something didn't feel right. Calista spent a week trying to clean the boat. But it somehow just didn't seem to look shipshape.

Dale had assured Mindy that everything would be OK. With his reassurances Mindy stifled her misgivings best as she could as she watched the boat pull away from the dock. Passing beneath the bridge he helped to build, Dale eased the *Magnum* out into the channel leading northeast out of Chiniak Bay. Off the starboard side was Woody Island which had once been the home of fox farms owned by the Russian American Fur Company. During the 19th century, they paid local Alutiiqs to operate the lucrative farms and harvest furs.

Off the port side was Spruce Cape, home to some of the most beautiful properties in Kodiak. Among these was the home of Doctor Bob.

Calista daydreamed briefly while looking out at Spruce Cape and her doctor's house. She had once been there for a family picnic. She remembered the house as looking like a ship on the inside. What she didn't know was that Doctor Bob and his wife Marion lived in the same house back in 1964 when the tidal wave hit. Calista knew from school that it was actually a tsunami, not a tidal wave. But the locals called it a tidal wave so that was good enough for her.

The disaster was caused by a massive 8.4 earthquake near Anchorage. Kodiak experienced a series of huge tidal surges. The Kodiak Harbor emptied several times. Each time a bigger surge returned. The devastation caused by the massive tidal wave was an unbelievable catastrophe. Some boats were torn to bits, while others were deposited in the middle of town. The shop foreman at Kodiak Electric sat on the roof of the shop and watched the whole thing. He was shocked by all the tires and junk that he saw laying on the harbor floor each time it emptied.

Doctor Bob's house sat about thirty feet off the channel and about 18 feet above the highest tide. The house survived the '64 wave. Now the *F/V Magnum* with the Pruitt family aboard passed by on their way to Buoy Four. This marked the place where they could safely turn west to head toward the fishing grounds. The crew milled around the boat performing needed tasks in order to get the ship ready for the thirteen hour trip across the Shelikof Strait. Mitchell went about his business quietly.

Cally asked, "Calista, you gonna get seasick?"

"No way!" she scoffed, "I've been out on the *Calista Marie* a million times and I've never been seasick. Besides, Dad won't let me get sick."

"OK, whatever, but I have a feeling you're gonna get sick." This drew a grin from Mitch, but that was it.

About one hour later, as the *F/V Magnum* was rounding Buoy Four and heading west past Fort Abercrombie and Monashka Bay, Calista Pruitt hung her head over the side and vomited. Her brother and cousin jeered at the site of her distress.

"You assholes!" She screamed between hurls. This, of course, led to more insults and rough teasing.

"I hate you guys! You suck!"

Calista brushed by Cally and Mitchell on her way into the cabin and her bunk. She lay down and fervently hoped to feel better or die. She was unaware at the time that she'd be sick for almost 48 hours before things would really get crazy.

Dale navigated the Ouzinkie Narrows, successfully heading west toward Whale Passage leading to the Kupreanof and Shelikof Straits. Kodiak is actually an archipelago consisting of Afognak, Raspberry, Whale, and Kodiak Islands among others. Whale Passage is a narrow corridor between Whale Island and Kodiak Island. Whale Passage and the Ouzinkie Narrows have some dangerous currents that have taken boats and their crews down over the years. Dale had navigated these waters many times. Once again he slipped through unscathed.

Fishermen and Alaskan ferries heading to the mainland from Kodiak commonly use Whale Passage and the Kupreanof Strait to cut between Kodiak and Afognak Islands, saving hours of time.

By the time the skipper guided the *F/V Magnum* from Kupreanof Strait into the Shelikof, his daughter had been continuously barfing for two hours. Of course, seasickness is not uncommon, especially for greenhorns, but this greenhorn was his daughter. He hoped she'd be O.K.

Cally, Calista, and Mitchell were in the cabin with Dale. The Magnum is a typical seiner with a forward cabin and an open deck on the stern. On the port side of the cabin was a small galley and a table edged by padded benches. To the starboard side of the small room was the skipper's chair forward, with a bunk directly behind it. Monitors, handsets, and cables surrounded the captain's chair.

The movie, *Cars* was playing on a small mounted monitor. Calista and Cally sat on the benches at the table and leaned back on pillows with their legs stretched lengthwise. They drifted in and out of the animated film. Conversation was difficult over the noise of the movie and the droning engines. Mitchell took watch while Dale made dinner. A taco feast was the customary first meal of any trip and this one was no different. With machine-like drive and precision borne of years of experience, the skipper diced tomatoes and onions and prepared a delicious Mexican meal in the swaying galley of the *Magnum* in the Shelikof Strait.

The seas in the Shelikof were moderate with three to four foot swells and 20-25 mph winds. Calista was miserable. She couldn't understand why she was so sick. This had never happened before and she'd been out in much worse conditions. She ate a few plain noodles and struggled to keep them down. She was sick, frustrated and complained profanely and loudly.

Once again Calista's irritability provided great entertainment for Mitch and Cally who laughed and jeered at yet another outburst from the kid.

"I hate you guys!" Calista then invented some new expletives and yelled at them at the top of her lungs.

"Mitchell, she's so mad she's making up swear words!" Cally said to Mitchell while the two cracked up. Calista mumbled a host of new creative words, expressing her extreme displeasure with her relatives' needling.

"Leave her alone, you two," Dale finally broke in. Even though he had also enjoyed a good chuckle at his daughter's expense, he knew she'd had enough. "Leave her alone."

Calista was grateful for her dad's intervention and quietly climbed back down to the bunks for another attempt at sleep. Dale hoped that she'd feel better. He needed her and these outbursts were not going to help the operation one bit. So he turned his attention to the watch order. He decided that Mitchell would be on duty first followed by Cally, Calista, and then himself.

*During the last century, two catastrophic events have greatly altered life on Kodiak Island. In 1912, Mt. Katmai erupted. This enormous volcanic explosion covered Kodiak Island with about two feet of volcanic ash. The fallout was powerful enough to destroy a number of houses and cause major respiratory problems for the hardy residents.*

*Some 50 years later, a cataclysmic earthquake occurred on Good Friday in 1964. It registered 8.4 on the Richter scale, making it the most powerful earthquake in modern North American history. It lasted for five minutes, creating massive fissures and several tsunamis. Numerous buildings were destroyed and 113 Alaskans lost their lives. The tsunamis caused damage as far away as Hawaii, Japan, and coastal towns in California.*

# CHAPTER FOUR

Mindy Pruitt still felt worried as she entered her empty home after work. Not having Dale at home was often the norm. Many years had seen him at sea for as long as ten months. Mindy and the kids, like other families in the industry, were used to two lives: one with Dad and one without. Somehow this felt different. This was more than just an empty house. She went to the kitchen and called Dale on his cell phone. There was no answer. If he were on the Calista Marie she could call him on the satellite (sat) phone, but she didn't know the Magnum's four digit 'sat' phone number. Cell phone service can be spotty for Kodiak fishermen outside of the harbor area. This many hours out, Mindy knew it was a long shot, but she tried anyway.

After a second attempt to reach him, Mindy left a message and hung up.

Walking into the kitchen she poured herself a healthy slug of cabernet. She put some leftover Crab Bisque in the microwave and waited for it to heat. She had made the bisque the night before for the send-off. She always liked the bisque better the second day. Everybody did.

She plopped on the couch with her dinner and grabbed the remote. Then she changed her mind and set it back down. She sat in the silence, ate her soup and drank the wine. The quiet felt good. She looked out the sliding glass door at the familiar view.

Mindy stared out at Island Lake, marveling at how it was something she hadn't done in years; to just sit and stare. She and Dale had done plenty of sitting out on the deck when they first finished building the house. She thought about the days before the house and the road. The one-room cabin next to the house is just off the water. That's where they lived in the early years. The hikes and canoe rides to the house with Dale were sweet memories.

Back then, hiking and canoeing provided the only access to their small cabin home. In 1989, they built the house. Dale and brother Rusty built the half-mile long road from the property to Lakeview Road. The road and the kids had changed everything. Mindy remembered fondly back to her early days with Dale. The adventure of establishing themselves on Kodiak Island had been endlessly exciting. The sweet little Washington girl had really done something wild, hadn't she? She'd left home to go live with a big, burly fisherman on the frontier. It had been a great move. She had never regretted it for a moment.

But on this night, Mindy felt lonely. She smiled to herself at the thought of it. Lonely. That was something that seldom happened in the Pruitt family. Life in the new house had never been boring. As Mitchell and Calista grew up, the house became like a small city full of friends and family. In the small community of Kodiak, everybody knows everybody and most are close. The Pruitt household has had an open door policy over the years. If a kid needed a place to eat or hang out for a few hours, Mitchell and Calista's house was where it was at.

Miss Mindy, or Warden Pruitt, as she had been so fondly referred to, was always there to make sure the kids had what they needed and behaved the way they should.

"Hugs and encouragement are mostly what they need," Mindy remembered saying often.

She sat on the couch for over an hour daydreaming about her family and the days before kids. Wine glass empty, she poured another and decided to make a couple of phone calls before going upstairs. She called her dear friend Robinette Sagalkin.

"Hi Robinette, it's Mindy"

"Well how are ya? Are they off?"

"Yep, looks like 'old Captain Dale has taken the kids off for a little bonding time." The sarcasm was not accidental.

"You o.k.?" Robinette said sensing an undercurrent of concern in Mindy's voice.

"You know Robinette, I'm fine. Thanks. Are you coming over Wednesday to get some of these ferns?"

"You got any wine left or should I bring a bottle?"


Mindy finished the dishes and headed up the stairs to her bedroom. The house had three stories. The main floor is in the middle. You enter the front door into a sitting room. A small bench is to the right, and shoes and boots are lying everywhere. In Kodiak, people don't wear shoes in the house. The rule is unwritten; just a local custom.

Adjacent to the sitting room is a large kitchen which is connected to the dining room on the other side. Straight ahead is the family room with two comfortable couches and an inviting large screen TV. Sliding glass doors lead to a large deck outside. The deck stretches around most of the house. The view from the Pruitt's deck is jaw-dropping. Island Lake is small, but with only about a dozen homes on its shores it seems as if Dale and Mindy have the lake to themselves. The kids have grown up kayaking and swimming in the summers and skating and snow machining in the winters. Indeed, this was great place to grow up.

In her room, Mindy finally relented and flipped on the TV. Paying little attention to what was on, she simply laid down in her bed and fell asleep. The TV was still blaring when she woke up at four in the morning.

On the *F/V Magnum*, Mitchell finished the first watch shift. He shook Cally awake to take her turn. Cally usually enjoyed being on watch. The solitude of a midnight watch shift was a welcome respite from the heavy labor and close quarters of life on a Kodiak salmon seiner. On this night however, she was antsy. She asked Mitchell to stay up with her for a while, which he did. Cally was uneasy, but she couldn't describe why so she kept her thoughts to herself. Mitchell eventually climbed the three steps down to his bunk and she was alone. She recalled the times that her mother had told her to always tell someone when she had one her premonitions. She said that if you tell someone when they happen they probably won't come true.

Nervously, Cally thought long about this as she guided the *Magnum* across the Shelikof Strait in the dead of night. This is dumb she thought, I'm not telling anyone. We're going to go out, catch some fish, make some money and go home. Then I'll be done with it. Before she knew it, her shift was over and she went down to gently nudge Calista awake for her shift. She felt bad about it because of the pain Calista was in. But Cally was tired too and knew she had a long hard day in front of her. Eventually Calista rallied from her bunk to take over. After getting her up to speed, Cally climbed down the stairs to her bunk and went to sleep.

At four in the morning, Calista was on watch. Her Dad was sleeping right next to her. Taylor Swift on her iPod distracted her from the pain she was in. Her head throbbed and she was woozy, but she hadn't thrown up yet since Cally woke her after her watch shift was over. She was sleepy and didn't know if she'd make it until 5:30 when her watch shift ended. She looked over at her dad sleeping in the Captain's bunk. She wanted so badly to sleep, but tried to tough it out. Dale needed the sleep too.

She stared at the computer screen. There was a small picture of the *F/V Magnum* moving on a line. Make sure it stays on the line and look for rocks and stuff, Calista thought to herself. Giving herself pep talks helped for about an hour when suddenly the familiar feeling in her stomach came again.

"Dad, I gotta puke!" She said as she ran out of the wheelhouse to the deck.

Dale rolled over toward the sound to see Calista charging out the door. Sighing heavily, he knew his sleep was over. He got up and took Calista's place at the controls. Minutes later she returned saying only, "thanks Dad". She lay down on the bench and tried for more sleep time.

As dawn began to break, Dale piloted the *F/V Magnum* past Cape Unalishagvak and Jute Bay and headed toward Portage Bay. The south coast of Portage Bay was where the crew hoped to find the fish.

Years of experience have taught fishermen like Dale Pruitt that salmon run south along the shores of the Katmai National Park on their way to the rivers of their birth. Not much is known about what the salmon do with their time out at sea, but their spawning patterns are quite predictable. Kodiak salmon seiners look for areas that provide a good lead. A lead is a section of coastline that juts out in the way of the migrating schools of fish, requiring them to swim around. It is in these lead areas that fishermen deploy their nets.

Dale settled the *F/V Magnum* within sight of the mainland half way between Kanatak Lagoon and the point at Cape Igvak. He rousted the crew to get up and get ready for work. He began to make breakfast. Eggs, bacon, and toast would provide the crew with the necessary protein fuel for the morning. Mitchell and Cally ate breakfast with Dale while Calista continued to moan down below.

"Dad, I don't feel good."

"You have to try to eat something dear."

"Yeah, it'll give you something to puke up next time," Mitchell chimed in sardonically.

"Thanks Mitch; appreciate it," Calista snapped back.

Calista emerged from the bunks, grabbed a bottle of water and slumped into the Captain's bunk located next to the controls.

Over breakfast, Dale gave the crew their marching orders.

"Cally, you work the floats. Calista you have leads." He glanced over to see that Calista's eyes were closed.

"Calista? You hear me?" She groaned and nodded.

Mitchell didn't need to be told what his job was. He would be skiff man. The most important crew job goes to the most experienced, able-bodied crew member. On the *Magnum*, that was Mitchell Pruitt.

Mitch had graduated from high school less than two weeks before. He wasn't your typical high school graduate. He exhibited a stoicism that belied his years. It seems to come with the territory in Kodiak. For whatever the reasons, the men who do this work seem to be a study in emotional understatement; never too high nor too low.

Mitchell played linebacker and fullback for the football team in high school. The football program was brand new and Mitchell and his team went to the state championship game in only their second year. The town was flush with Bear Fever and the feeling was great for Mitch and friends like Clyde Valdez, Ben Watkins, and Mike Holden. Clyde and Ben would be going with Mitchell to college in California in the fall. Mike had graduated early and was already in the Coast Guard.

Dale was still talking to the crew, but Mitchell was daydreaming about how his buddies were just as much Miss Mindy's kids as he was. His mom was just that way; so full of love that she had plenty for everybody. There had been numerous times growing up when Mitch's mom or dad came to the rescue of one of his buddies. Mitchell loved this about his parents and was smiling slightly when his dad broke through his inattention.

"Mitch, get the skiff ready."

"Okay, Dad." Mitchell put his plate in the sink, (dishes were not in his job description) put on his rain gear, and headed out to the stern to begin his day's work.

Mindy Pruitt's head was throbbing when she woke on Tuesday morning. Her uneasy feelings of the previous night were still present. She lay awake thinking about the kids until 5:30.

She dragged herself out of bed and into the shower. Warm water felt good, and the morning cup of coffee had her up and ready to go. She was in front of the office by 7:00.

"Good Morning Miss Mindy!" The greeting came from the children playing in front of the Family Investment Center.

"Did you hear about the bear?" asked a seven year old Alutiiq boy.

"I did honey. Officer Holden came down and scared him away so I think we're going to be okay. Now you have a good day."

"Okay Miss Mindy. Bye!"

Mindy walked into the Family Investment Center of the Kodiak Housing Authority. This recreation hall had been built with federal grants written by Mindy and others. She worked for the local authority that provided low income housing to locals. Many of her clients are native descendants of the Alutiiqs. Kodiak is a culturally diverse area with Caucasian, Native American, and Asian people making up most of the population. Mindy's organization provides housing assistance and support to low income residents. Her family center has a game room, computer room, library, kitchen, and basketball courts for kids in the public housing projects.

Buoyed by her morning greeting from the kids out front, Mindy settled down to her desk and went to work. A busy day mostly kept her mind off Dale and the kids. She didn't think too much about them until she got back home to the house that evening. Once again, the feeling of emptiness returned.

This night was different though. Her children completely filled her thoughts. Images of Calista working on the boat and fighting with her brother came and went. She smiled inwardly. She knew that Mitchell and Calista truly loved one another, but *boy could they scrap.* The fighting between the kids was hard for her to take sometimes, but it usually blew over quickly.

Afterwards, Mindy would often hear a soft *I love you Mitchell* from her room across the hall.

A pause and then, *I love you too Calista*, usually followed.

She thought long thoughts about the kids growing up and spent the rest of the evening trying to relax. She bustled around cleaning the house (her way of relaxing) until she was tired out and laid down to sleep.

# SEWARD'S FOLLY

*A key figure in the history of Alaska and Kodiak Island was William Seward, the famous unsuccessful candidate for the U. S. presidency. During his tenure as Secretary of State for Abraham Lincoln, he was a staunch abolitionist.*

*On April 14, 1865, William Powell, one of John Wilkes Booth's assassination plot participants, strode up to Seward's home. Powell entered the house and climbed the stairs where he was met by Seward's son, Frederick. He pistol-whipped Frederick and then stabbed Seward with a bowie knife. He was captured the next day and eventually executed for his misdeeds.*

*Luckily for Seward, he was wearing a neck brace which probably saved his life. Fortunately, he recovered enough to negotiate a piece of 1867 legislation which would make the United States one of the largest nations in the world. The 586,412 square miles of Alaskan land which was purchased by the United States cost about two cents an acre and was twice the size of Texas.*

*At the time, Seward was vilified for his purchase of Alaska. The action was sometimes characterized as "Seward's*

*Folly and "Seward's Icebox." But the gold discoveries during the late 1800s and the later oil discoveries proved the critics wrong. For the next 92 years Alaska remained a "Territory".*

# CHAPTER FIVE

Inside the cabin of the *Magnum,* Cally worked her way into brand new rain gear. She looked over at her younger cousin and felt for her. Calista was hurting and had been for about 14 hours.

"You ready for this?"

"No, I'm still sick."

"Well get your stuff on, maybe the work will help."

Calista mumbled incoherently as they continued to get ready.

Outside, standing atop a four foot pile of net and line piled on the deck of the Magnum, Mitchell paused to look out at Cape Igvak which was less than a half-mile away. It was extremely rugged terrain.

It took Mitch two leaps to bound from the net-pile on the stern of the *Magnum* into the skiff. He readied the silver open-bow boat and waited for Calista and Cally to get ready.

Cape Igvak is foggy and windy most of the time. This day was no different. Mitchell smiled to himself. He had been waiting for this moment his whole life; first mate, under his father's command. They weren't on the *Calista Marie*, but this old piece of junk would have to do. Dale's seine sat in a lumpy mound on the stern of the *Magnum*. From his vantage point in the skiff, Mitchell could barely see his father at the wheel in the cabin. He relished the moment as he strained to see the signal from his dad. His moment of solitude aboard the skiff of *F/V Magnum* was short lived as his little sister came stumbling out of the cabin fumbling to get her raingear on. She appeared to be trying to tell Mitchell something, but there would be no way to hear over the engine noise in the skiff. So Mitchell jumped from the skiff back onto the stern of the Magnum landing near the struggling Calista.

"This sucks! Mitchell! Help me get this on"

"Get it on yourself; I have to get the skiff ready."

"Thanks Mitch, you're very helpful. I'm puking my guts out, the weather sucks, this place sucks. I hate this. Thanks again Mitch," she said spitefully.

"Here's Dad's black tape." He grabbed a roll of black, electrical tape that was spooled on a hook just outside the cabin door. "When you get your jacket on over your gloves, roll the tape tight around your sleeves like this." He stuck an arm out to show her his technique.

"You know Mitchell, I've been out with Dad. I've seen that before you know." Calista sneered, incredulous that he would think her so stupid. She continued her litany of complaints as Mitch turned away.

Mitchell shook his head, ignoring her rant, as he jumped back to the skiff for the first set of the day. They were here to catch some fish. With his dad at the helm and he in the skiff, these fish were toast. He was waiting for the signal from Dale, and was happy that he couldn't hear his sister's bellyaching over the drone of the jet skiff engine.

Mitch looked at the rugged Alaskan mainland from his perch. This land looked as if it were made yesterday. Mountains appeared to explode out of the ground. Sheer, treeless rock cliffs rose sharply up from the water. He didn't notice any beach area.

He was greatly energized, but his enthusiasm would be short lived as the young crew struggled that day. Salmon seining is an age-old technique. It's challenge fishing at its best. But the crew was green and the fishing was less than spectacular. The first day with a new crew can be that way. Throw in a sick teenager and you have more problems. A veteran crew can run a full set in about 30 minutes. Dale Pruitt's crew struggled to complete one per hour.

The F/V *Magnum* had towed the skiff from her stern on the trip to Cape Igvak. Mitchell untied the safety line that he had secured before they left port. Dale taught Mitchell to always lash an extra line to the skiff so as not to lose it en route. In addition to the safety line, the skiff is secured to the boat with a quick release lever called a *pancake*. It's this pancake that fisherman use in action. The skiff man can jump in, attach the seine to the tow tower, and fire it up. A crewmember on deck then releases the skiff with a simple pull of a lever on the pancake. With the safety line removed Mitch was ready.

Dale was training his new crew. After being set, the seine would be pulled through a pulley system called the block. Attached to the boom, the block is raised to a height of about 15 feet above the deck.

To get the net out in the water, Mitchell would pull it from the stern of the seiner using the skiff. Once set and secured, the crew would have a little break while the net did its work. (Calista was already dreaming of her thirty-minute break) Mitchell would gradually bring the skiff around and circle back toward the *Magnum*. When the seine had been set for about 30 minutes the crew would use the deck winch to pull the seine back onto the deck of the *F/V Magnum*. As the net started coming in, Cally and Calista would be busy stacking floats and leads respectively.

Dale went through the routine with them again. He wasn't sure how this was going to work out. Calista was in a bad mood. She still didn't feel good and her irritability was evident. Dale knew he was in for a long day. It was 6 a.m. off of Cape Igvak on Tuesday, June 19th when Mitchell Pruitt led the skiff away from *F/V Magnum* to make the first set of the day.

Thirteen hours and eight sets later they would call it a day. The fishing had been slow. With an experienced crew, Dale usually made around twenty sets in a day of fishing. But considering the situation he was happy with what they had accomplished. Calista once again was in her bunk trying to sleep away the sickness as they approached the tender.

Salmon seiners out of Kodiak are limited to a length of 58 feet in order to protect small owner/operators. This maximum-sized boat is called a "limit seiner". Because the boats are relatively small, their fish holds are limited in capacity. Instead of having to make the thirteen hour journey all the way back to offload fish in Kodiak, the canneries send boats called tenders out to where the seiners are operating. These tenders are much larger boats with larger holds. Often times

Bering Sea crab boats double as tenders during the off-crab season. Using the tender system, seiners are able to fish and off-load on site and then return to fish some more. Tenders then run back and forth to the canneries with holds full of salmon.

Dale didn't expect to offload that evening since they had only 3000 pounds of salmon aboard. That amount could easily be kept fresh in his fish hold and included with the next day's catch. The tender captain had radioed and informed him that cannery boss Tim Blott had called. He wanted him to bring his catch on in. This was the plan when Dale pulled up alongside the *Lucrative*. The crews of both boats worked together to secure the *Magnum* to the anchored tender. Mitchell, Cally, and a reluctant, cranky Calista moved from the *Magnum* to the tender and began sorting through the fish.

A large boom on the stern of the *Lucrative* held a sinewy vacuum hose. One end of the hose was open; and the other was connected to machinery aboard the tender. The open end of the giant fish vacuum tube was lowered toward the fish hold of the *Magnum*. Dale was the only remaining crew member aboard the Magnum. He grabbed the open vacuum tube as it inched down from the larger boat toward him. With the help of a *Lucrative* crewmember at the boom controls, Dale gently guided the tube through the opening in the deck and into the watery hold containing the day's catch. A flip of a switch on the vacuum machine caused a powerful shifting of the tube as it dangled overhead and into the fish hold. Shifting and shaking, the machine quickly began its work of sucking 3000 pounds of fish from out of the *Magnum's* hold over to a large metal sorting table anchored to the large aft deck of the tender boat. Gradually, large, beautiful silvery salmon began to spill from within the machinery; sliding easily onto a large sorting table. Gravity gently pushed the fish down the angled table toward the scale, before being hung up on a metal gate. Along the way, crewmembers, standing on either side of the table, sort out reds and silvers and toss them into bins located on deck. The remaining Humpies (pink salmon) start to pile up at the gate until there's no room for more. At this time, the system is stopped and the accumulation of fish is weighed and recorded. The gate is then reopened to allow the load to spill down toward the deck of the *Lucrative*. The fish are then scooped into the fish hold below deck through a circular opening. This hatch sits just a couple of inches higher than the 33 degree water in the fish hold. The salmon on deck quickly disappear, and the process repeats itself.

The greenhorn crew quickly learned that the tender captains watch carefully while you're sorting. Calista was yelled at for slipping humpies into the red salmon bin. Of course, reds paid about 97 cents a pound, considerably more than the humpies brought.

As the *F/V Magnum* pulled away from the tender, the *Lucrative's* crew noticed a pronounced starboard list to the boat. The crew of the *F/V Cape Clear* noticed the same list. The *Cape Clear* was the next seiner in line waiting to deliver fish to the tender. Aboard the *Cape Clear,* Guy Costello grabbed his camera and took a picture. The ominous photo he took foreshadowed the danger to come. Aboard the *Magnum,* Captain Dale Pruitt attributed the list to water shifting in the holds. He didn't like the boat (no one did) but he felt that in spite of the list, the boat was worthy of another day's fishing. They headed back toward the fishing grounds.

Dale anchored the *Magnum* just off of Cape Igvak near Kanatak Lagoon. He had spent many a night anchored in Kanatak Lagoon in his fishing years, but on this night he didn't go in. The lagoon provides excellent anchorage during an on-shore blow, but the wind was coming off shore on this night and there was no need. Dale made spaghetti for dinner and the tired crew wolfed it down. Calista, again, went to her bunk without eating. She had gone thirty hours without food. All she could think of was getting home, getting off this boat. She never wanted to see another fish as long as she lived.

# MODERN KODIAK

*Kodiak Island is a sport fisherman's dream; but it's also a commercial fisherman's livelihood. The island is perfectly suited both for pleasure and commercial fishing. It has unexpectedly high mountain peaks, along with plenty of rain, rushing rivers, and the surrounding ocean waters. This combination of elements makes for outstanding salmon fishing. These fish fight their way upstream, scoop out nests in the sand at the bottom of the river, lay their eggs and die within a few days. The Pacific Salmon runs are one of the main sources of revenue for commercial fishermen.*

*But in addition to the Pacific salmon runs, Pacific halibut and crab are also abundant and comprise an additional part of the industry along with plentiful supplies of king crab. The Kodiak Grizzly Bear is one of the island's native land animals. Kodiak residents are also involved in other commercial enterprises such as logging and ranching. Moreover, the island has a number of canneries for fish processing.*

*So with all these features, as one can see, this island is a land for adventurous, hard-working people. Dale and Mindy Pruitt and their family were good examples of the industrious, sea-going Alaskans who make their home on Kodiak Island. The Pruitt's harrowing adventure seems to represent the potential hazards that all fishermen must endure in order to make a living by satisfying the palates of seafood gourmets.*

# CHAPTER SIX

It was 4 A.M. on Wednesday, June 20th when Mindy woke. She reached for the remote and turned off the TV. She lay in bed thinking of her family. This home-alone stuff would take some getting used to. Her mind drifted between a sinking feeling of dread that her daughter needed her and confidence in her husband's ability as a seaman.

*This is the way we do things here in Kodiak*, she told herself. *It's how we live.*

It helped when she thought of how good Dale was at what he did. *Not a chance in Hell he'll let anything happen to those kids.*

Mindy lay in bed for another hour before getting up and brewing some coffee. Another busy day at work would be good; something to get her mind off her family at sea.

The Pruitt's second day of fishing in the Shelikof Strait was underway. The crew was improving and so was the weather. The winds were still blowing 20 to 30 miles per hour out of the southwest; perfect weather for this country. Dale and crew were finishing the day's work and had brought in about 10,000 pounds of red and pink salmon. Not a huge take for a fisherman like Dale, but a big improvement over the 3,000 pounds that they had delivered to the *Lucrative* the night before. They were able to make three or four more sets and Dale was happy with the way the crew was shaping up.

Calista was still in bad shape. She had spent much of the day in her dad's bunk. "Get out of my bunk with those nasty clothes," he had barked.

"Dad I don't feel good."

Dale left her alone. The call to Mindy on the previous night had reminded him that Calista had experienced other health issues in the past.

*Dale, you need to bring her home tomorrow if she doesn't start eating and drinking. Her kidneys, Dale.*

Calista had a history of kidney problems. They had once come close to failure. Her mom always kept a close eye on her health. She knew that being sick that long was especially bad for Calista; she worried.

*Dale you need to bring her home.* Dale was thinking about the conversation when the last set of the day was being brought around.

He yelled to her, "Calista, get out there and get those leads! Mitchell's just about around."

Calista dragged herself out of her dad's bunk onto the deck of the *Magnum*. Dale had given some thought about their next move. He decided then that he would talk to the crew about what to do and let them vote. He had a strong hunch that Cally and Mitch had heard enough of Calista's whining. They were ready to go home. On another level, Calista's ill health also nagged at Dale because of her previous history. He thought he knew what the verdict would be. It was close to eight in the evening on Thursday when they finished bringing the final load of salmon aboard. Dale called the crew into the wheelhouse.

"Hey guys, you want to offload these fish here or do you want to take 'em back to Kodiak?" Dale asked. "We can get about an extra thousand if we take it home which would be about a hundred each for you guys."

"I want to go home and take a shower." Calista was the first to speak up, surprising no one. "I'm sick. I want to go home and see Mom".

Cally and Mitchell didn't put up any arguments. Both were tired of hearing her constant complaining.

They really did feel for her since they knew she was feeling rotten. Dale also knew that James would be back from football camp, ready to go out on the next trip. The original plan had been to drop off Cally and pick up James on the return. Now it looked like he might have to talk Cally into taking Calista's place. He was pretty sure he wasn't going to have to fire his daughter. He could tell she had no more interest in commercial fishing. He mainly felt good about Mitchell and Cally's work. He hoped he could persuade Cally to stay on for the summer. Otherwise, he'd have to look elsewhere. The decision to return to Kodiak that night brought a sense of relief to the *Magnum's* crew. That relief paled in comparison to the joy the news brought Mindy back home.

"Hi sweetheart; we're going to come home."

"How long will it take?" Mindy tried to contain her excitement.

"Sixteen hours. We'll see you tomorrow."

"How's Calista? Has she eaten anything?"

"She's fine dear; we'll see you tomorrow afternoon. I love you."

Dale had avoided the question which Mindy knew meant that her daughter needed her.

"I love you too. Get those kids home safe."

"And get me home safe too?"

"Yes, get yourself home safe too!"

In the wheelhouse of the *F/V Magnum,* Dale Pruitt hung up the satellite phone. The phone looked more like a walkie talkie. But it's a godsend for the fleet to communicate with their families back home.

The crew secured the nets and used the pancake to fasten the skiff to the stern for the long tow to Kodiak. In addition, Dale instructed Mitchell to tie the skiff to the Magnum with an extra safety line. From years of hard-won experience, Dale used his own safety precautions. He never trusted the pancake alone to hold the skiff in rough seas. Dale was giving Mitch the benefit of his knowledge when he explained that many fishermen have lost skiffs under tow in bad weather.

With the Magnum headed toward home, Dale checked the cabin around him. Over by the sink Calista was sipping a 7-Up. *So I'll have something to puke up.* The rest of the exhausted crew had already crawled into their bunks below. Both Cally and Mitchell knew that their watch session would be coming soon enough. They wanted to get as much sleep as possible. Calista lay down in the Captain's bunk in the wheelhouse once again. This drew a smile from her dad who couldn't bring himself to make her move. At least she was dry this time.

He had a *following sea* (what fishermen call going with the current) at his back of three to four foot swells. The winds were hitting his starboard stern at 20-30 miles per hour, blowing out of the southwest through the Shelikof Strait. Not too bad. He intended to travel *up the line* (along the coastline) on the mainland due west past Jute Bay and Cape Unalishagvak. When he reached that point he would cut over through the main channel of the Strait across to Kodiak Island. When he reached the island on the other side, he would make his way back through Kupreanof Strait, Whale Passage, and the Ouzinkie Narrows to reach home port in Kodiak on the eastern side of the Island. This was a well crafted plan, consistent with their present location.

He missed his agile little boat, the *Calista Marie*. She was smaller; much more responsive. He had made this run hundreds of times in all types of crazy weather in the trusty *Calista Marie*. The *F/V Magnum*, on the other hand, was a big, tank-heavy metal boat.

The fact that he and his crew had reservations about this boat was a no-brainer. There was fishing to be done and bills to be paid. Dale would fight through the summer with this boat. The price of Salmon was up. If they had a good summer, they would be able to find a new boat for the next season. He was fishing with his family. Even though he knew Calista was done, he didn't mind.

Dale knew that he'd spend the rest of the summer fishing with his son, his nephew and maybe his niece. That brought him a feeling of deep satisfaction.

At 10:15 on Wednesday, June 20th, Dale Pruitt felt settled about what was to come. In the solitude of the wheelhouse, tired crew resting, he was happy. Like most moments in the commercial fishing industry however, this was not to last. Dale noticed that the weather was changing.

Mindy, still anxious at the house, felt for the first night since Monday that she might get some sleep. She thought about the day to come as she tried to relax in bed. She would work as usual in the morning and take the afternoon off. She planned to have her friend Tanya help her drop off the truck at the cannery for Dale and the kids so they'd have transportation home.

She would go to one of her usual spots to watch for the boat. Should she go to Spruce Cape or Near Island to look out for them? She wasn't sure, but she could work that out tomorrow. She would also run to the store to get Calista all of her favorite things, beginning with cranberry-pomegranate juice.

Mindy knew that she loved juice and that she'd need to start hydrating her. She was ready to have Calista home. Once again her racing mind made sleep impossible. Mindy got out of bed and started cleaning Calista's bathroom. She finally gave up and went back to bed at around midnight. She slept well that night knowing she'd see her family the next day. What she didn't know was that when her head hit the pillow that night the *F/V Magnum* was already in big trouble.

# CHAPTER SEVEN

About an hour into the return trip, Dale was struggling with the cantankerous helm. He was a mile or so south of Jute Bay to his port side as he traveled east. The unpredictable winds from the peninsula and Bristol Bay, feared by every Kodiak fisherman, were blowing at gale force. The worst possible conditions had developed for the fisherman.

Friend and fellow fisherman, Clint Johnson, was several miles ahead of Dale on a similar run back to town. Dale decided to call him.

"Clint where are you?"

"Hey Dale, it's getting really nasty out here. Everything OK with you guys?"

"No. This weather's shitty and I can't get this damned boat to do anything. Where are you and what's happening?"

"Well, we just ducked back around Unalishagvak. It's a little better over here. Think we'll just try to work our way up the line and then cross farther north. Otherwise, just duck into cover and find anchorage and wait this thing out. You think you can get her over here?"

"Yeah we're good Clint. I'm going to take her off auto and head on in. I'm not too far out so it shouldn't be a problem. I'll talk to you tomorrow."

"Alright Dale, take care. See you back home."

With strong gusts now battering the boat's port side Dale switched off the auto pilot and struggled to turn into the wind. Huge waves hammered them relentlessly. The boat fought him at every move of the wheel. Unable to keep steady into the wind he fought back. He cursed the vessel roundly. Time to take action. They were in serious trouble.

The portside waves had pounded the *F/V Magnum* into a 45 degree starboard list. He yelled to the crew to wake up and get their survival suits on. Calista, trying to sleep in Dale's bunk right next to him, was the first to respond. She stumbled to the closet where the suits were kept and threw one each to Cally and Mitchell. She draped Dale's over the back of his captain's chair.

Dale yelled to Mitchell to move the heavy steel boom on the deck (*vang the boom*). Mitchell rushed out of the cabin to the deck. He balanced the boat's weight by moving the boom from the starboard side to the port side. This action brought temporary leveling to the boat. Inside, Calista and Cally struggled panic stricken into their survival suits. Calista just managed to get her suit on when she spotted the flashing red light under the cabinet near Dale's legs. When Dale realized it was the lazarette alarm he knew things had taken a very ominous turn.

Dale ignored entreaties to get his survival suit on as he continued to fight with the controls. Shifting the boom had not solved the problem and the frightening list had returned.

The lazarette is an air compartment in the stern of a fishing boat. It exerts a strong influence on the stability of a vessel. If it's full of water the consequences are dire. Lazarette alarms are required on commercial fishing boats. The *Magnum* had one, but the audio portion of the alarm had malfunctioned. The crew's plight suddenly became life-threatening. If the lazarette alarm had sounded, Dale would probably have been able to maneuver the boat to safety. As it was, the plight of the Magnum's crew was rapidly becoming desperate.

Tools began to fly around the wheelhouse. Frigid ocean water was rushing in through an open window. Past time to abandon ship. Dale yelled to the crew to get into the skiff. They would use the small boat to run the mile or so to shore and then wait for someone to rescue them. In the midst of all this chaos, Dale's mind was clear. Functioning clearly he knew what needed to be done, but time was short. *F/V Magnum* was going down fast and he knew it. They needed to get into that skiff and away from the boat yesterday.

"Out of the boat!"

"Where do I go dad?" Calista shrieked.

"In the skiff, get in the skiff!"

The crew struggled to climb up to the door leading out to the deck. Calista and Cally frantically clawed their way up the floor of the 90 degree tilting cabin. Debris flying through the cabin struck them as they climbed. They reached the cabin door together when another large wave jolted the boat, knocking them both out of the door into the cold water filling up the deck. Tumbling onto the deck, Cally struck her head on the steel winch before she came to rest squarely on top of Calista. For a brief moment, Calista's head was submerged.

The head blow and the force of the fall caused Cally to then slip off the deck, over the now submerged gunwale, and into the icy Shelikof Strait. A tangled mess of lines was around her neck. She panicked. Amid the chaos, she had only been able to get her survival suit zipped to her chest. Her head was exposed. The suit immediately began to fill with numbing water. When the suits are on correctly, they double as flotation devices. A half-zipped suit will fill with water. Maneuvering becomes a nightmare. Cally's adrenaline surged as she struggled in the tangle of lines. She felt no pain from the head blow or the freezing water. Physical pain wasn't her biggest immediate problem. Her biggest problem was her full-blown mindless panic.

She flailed at the lines, shrieking when she came up for air. Churning water around her head and face swallowed most of the available breathing space. Cally finally managed to free herself from the lines. She began to drift.

"Cally!" Calista screamed as she scrambled up to the dry portion of the deck. She could see Cally in the ocean water. She shouted at her frantically. "Swim toward the boat! Swim toward the damn boat!" Calista could see Cally was drifting away into the darkness. At this time she saw Mitchell climbing out of the doorway to the deck. Inside the cabin, Dale was yelling "Mayday, Mayday; this is *F/V Magnum* two miles off of Unalishagvak in distress".

"Dad! Get out of there! It's gonna roll!"

Dale waited a quick moment at the radio for a reply. No answer. He realized it was past time to exit the wheelhouse. It was filling fast. The time for another mayday call had just run out. He had to get out now. Dale grabbed his survival suit and sloshed his way to the door.

Mitchell turned to see his dad standing at the door to the wheelhouse, suit in hand.

"Come on Dad, Cally's in the water! We have to get her!" Calista yelled frantically.

"Move! Let's go. Cally hang onto one of those lines!" He yelled to his struggling niece as he made his way to the skiff boat.

The stacked seine on the stern of the boat had begun to spill out in the sea as Dale clambered over the high side pile of net toward the stern. Mitchell was already in the skiff. Calista reached a hand to her brother and he pulled her aboard. A strong tug of the pancake by Dale was all he needed to release the skiff and jump aboard. His plan was ready. This was now a rescue mission. Take the skiff, run over to pick up Cally, head to shore. That was Dale's take on what had to be done. The weather was bad and he wasn't sure they'd make it, but at this point his choices were limited and his desperation drove him on. Dale pulled the quick release on the pancake and jumped in. He landed in the skiff with a sudden jolt. He lost his balance and fell heavily, causing the skiff to rock wildly. Mitchell and Calista had to brace themselves aboard the small boat to keep it steady. Unfortunately for the crew though, the pancake release lever did not release the skiff from the foundering *Magnum*.

"Dammit! The safety line. Mitchell, do you have a knife to cut that thing?

"No Dad! I don't have my knife."

The safety line Mitchell had tied to ensure the skiff wouldn't break free on the deadhead home held them fast to the sinking fishing boat. Mitch felt responsible. A veteran first mate would have a knife at the ready. He jumped from the skiff back to the nearly submerged deck of the Magnum and tried to find his way back to the cabin to retrieve his knife.

"Mitchell! You retard! Don't go in there!"

Calista was the greenhorn on this trip, but she knew enough about fishing to know that the last place you want to be when a boat rolls is in the wheelhouse. Her mom had told her that Captains often went down with the ship because they're in the wheelhouse getting a mayday out when the boat rolls. This boat was about to roll. Calista had no desire to see her brother go with it. Mitchell peeked into the wheelhouse, thought better of it, and came back to the skiff.

Lacking a knife, Dale and Mitchell struggled briefly trying to untie the line. But the wind's force, the wetness of the line, and the fact that the *Magnum* was rolling over closed down that effort. The skiff began to list along with the rolling of the fishing vessel.

Meanwhile, Cally held on against the wind and current in the darkness.

The force of the winds and current quickly rolled the *Magnum*. The momentum of the turtling vessel was rolling the skiff over with it as well. Dale had to act fast or they'd all be in the water.

"Jump over to the hull!"

"What?"

"Jump to the hull! We can get on top of it!"

He climbed over to the bottom of the Magnum now bobbing upside down in the waves. He saw debris floating around and could still see and hear Cally floating about 50 feet away in the freezing water.

"Swim over here Cally!"

"I can't Uncle Dale. It's too hard. I'm tired. I'm letting go. I'm too tired."

"You have to! Get your butt over here!"

As Dale steadied himself atop the Magnum's hull, he turned back to see Mitchell making his way as well. He never saw Calista although she was behind Mitchell desperately climbing toward safety. He reached to give a hand up to his son when a massive wave slammed Mitchell and Calista into the ocean.

Captain Dale Pruitt gathered himself into a wide stance for balance and assessed his situation. He had just called his wife one hour ago. It had been less than ten minutes since he called his friend Clint Johnson. He had just put out a mayday. In the turmoil, he had lost his survival suit. (Most likely the suit had gone over with the skiff) He was standing on the bottom side of his sinking fishing boat. The wind was blowing ferociously. The wind chill was factor was in the 20s. The water temperature was 47 degrees. He was wearing a t-shirt, shorts and flip flops. It was getting dark and visibility was minimal.

And his children were in the water.

The force of the wave that knocked the kids into the water was unlike anything Mitchell had ever felt. He had taken a lot of hard hits playing high school football, but none of them came close to this one.

It took a moment for Mitchell and Calista to recover their wits in the water. When they did, Calista panicked and tried to climb back up onto the sloping hull. She spotted a large floating box nearby, reached out and grabbed onto it, wiggling her way to the top of it. Mitchell looked over and thought she looked like a fishing bobber in the water.

Meanwhile, downwind Cally was hanging on by a thread. The line Uncle Dale told her to grab was her savior so far. When she first grabbed it, the currents and wind were too powerful and she couldn't hang on. But grabbing the line strong with both hands, she was able to turn her body away from the sinking boat and pull it over her shoulder. Holding on for dear life, Cally struggled to keep herself from being swept away. With two hands on the line facing away from the *Magnum* Cally Rose Pruitt thought about death. Meanwhile, the shouting of her family behind her was growing fainter now.

*Cally come over here! Get over here! Swim Cally, swim over here!* She could hear her panicked family behind her. They had their hands full back at the sinking ship, but never lost track of Cally Rose bobbing in the sea.

Cally began to have visions of her mother Nancy, father Jeff, and boyfriend Isaac, while strong cold waves slapped at her and made it hard to breath. She was swallowing large mouthfuls of sea water. She wasn't sure she could hang on. She was crying out for somebody, anybody to help her.

From atop the hull of the Magnum, Dale heard his daughter's voice in the water.

"Dad, I'm floating on this thing!"

"What?"

"I'm floating on this box!"

Instantly he recognized that what Calista was floating on was the life raft; still in its box. Dale suddenly knew what he had to do. Death from hypothermia comes quickly when one is floating unprotected in 47 degree water. Dale cared little about this fact when he jumped into the Shelikof Strait. He knew only that his family was at risk. The shock of the water drilled to his core. His legs became instantly numb. His thoughts were centered on the rescue of the kids. He started swimming toward his daughter as she rode out a large dark swell aboard her bulky float.

"Dad, it says to pull here."

Dale heard Calista as he moved toward her in the water, but his eyes were fixed on Cally off in the distance. Then he saw that Mitchell was swimming out to where his cousin was stranded.

"Hold on."

"Where's Mitchell going?" Calista asked Dale who had made his way over to where she was still clinging to the bobbing box that contained the life raft.

"He's going to get Cally. Come on! Let's get this damn thing open."

Meanwhile, Cally was losing hope. She hadn't drifted any further from the boat since she had been able to pull the line over her shoulder and hang on. But her strength was waning. The cold made her think about letting go.

Cally's life was hanging in the balance. Thoughts of her grandfather pushing her on the swings as a child drifted across her mind.

Weakly, she was yelling goodbyes to her family members back at the boat when she felt a hand on her shoulder. Panicked, she began to thrash and fight with her rescuer.

She eventually quit struggling. Mitchell was able to drag her back toward the boat where Calista and Dale continued to wrestle with the box that held their only hope. The raft is designed to open upon hitting the water, but that feature had malfunctioned. One more life-threatening equipment screw-up.

Mitchell got back to the capsized vessel and tossed Cally a line. He then quickly covered the short distance to where Calista and Dale were clinging to the bobbing cube. The *sea painter* (the line connecting the life raft to the main vessel) is 100 feet long. Dale started at the hydro release that connects the sea painter to the *F/V Magnum* and ran the 100 feet of line through his hands until reaching the point where it attaches to the box containing the raft. It was there that the compressed oxygen container was found. That would instantly deploy the survival vessel.

Working his best to gain leverage in the frigid Shelikof, Dale gave a few quick yanks to the line. He paid no attention to the fact that his body was seizing up. The box didn't open. He kept working desperately despite the fact that death in the icy water was very close.

In their various stages of survival suit dress/undress, the kids might last for several hours. But for Dale Pruitt, as he grappled with the malfunctioning life raft, hypothermia and death would be upon him post haste if he was unable to open that box.

"Mitchell! Help me pull this!"

Mitchell slid his way over from the other side of the box. With his dad on one side and him on the other, they yanked on that line with a strength that neither knew they had. Finally, a loud pop was followed by a hissing sound. The oxygen tank did its job. The raft inflated in a matter of seconds. They had been in the ocean for about twenty minutes, and now their chances had improved exponentially. Dale had become completely numb and knew he had to get out of the water as quickly as possible.

"Oh Dad, it's upside down!"

In the dark Alaskan night it had been hard to see that the raft was upside down in the water. The good news for the crew was that the raft was still tethered by the sea painter to the capsized *F/V Magnum*. If they hadn't been attached, the intense winds would likely have scattered them about. As it was, they were able to stay close together by hanging first on to the box, and then to the raft.

The crew and the raft were downwind from the foundering vessel. The 100 foot sea painter line was taut now and strong winds were bearing down on them from the southwest. On the leeward side of the life raft, Dale and Mitchell pushed with all their strength. Leverage was difficult, if not impossible and the wind answered any challenge offered up by pushing the raft right back at them. Father and son struggled for survival in this fashion for a minute or two before Calista suggested using the wind to help.

"You guys get on the other side and the wind will help you!"

Dale and Mitchell worked their way around to the other side of the raft. Meanwhile, Cally had a chicken wing hold on the sea painter line and was in bad shape.

"Uncle Dale I'm tired and cold."

"Yeah, we all are, Cally, hang on."

Now on the windward side of the raft Mitchell and Dale started to push again. With the wind at the men's backs, the force of Dale and Mitchell pushing from down in the water caused the raft to slowly tip over. They saw that the raft looked like a floating pup tent. The base of the raft was like any raft they had seen, but this one had a tent covering it that began to open as the weight of the water drained off of it. The only one downwind of the raft now, Calista worked her way around to the windward side to where the rest of her family now looked up. They discussed their next move.

"Let's go Cally, time to get out of this water."

"I can't Dale, I'm too full of water and I'm too tired."

Dale grabbed Cally Rose and struggled to get her over to the opening. Cally, most likely in shock at this point, fought with her uncle.

"I can't get in there Dale! It's too high and I'm full......"

"Dammit Cally," Calista interrupted, "get in the life raft or we're gonna die out here! Dad you need to get in there first. You're the only one without a suit on. You have to get out of this damned water now."

"Yeah Dad," chimed in Mitchell, "you get up there and then you can help her. I'll push from down here."

In spite of the terrible situation, the crew began operating as if it had been preparing for this for a lifetime. Despite all of the odds and the horror that had occurred since the boat capsized, they were alive and working like a team. They knew what they had to do. As Captain, Dale was reluctant to get up in the raft first. As dad, his instinct was to get everybody in and then save himself if possible. But he knew that Calista and Mitchell were right. There would be no getting Cally into the raft without someone pulling from up above. He chose not to fight their plan and after twenty-five to thirty minutes in the boreal waters of Alaska, Dale decided to climb into the life raft.

He figured that if this plan didn't work he could always jump back in. He knew then that he wouldn't be going home without all of the kids safe. If he was to see Mindy again it would be with all of the kids. He'd never be able to face her if he lost one of them.

Climbing in was difficult. The inflatable pontoons of the raft raised its deck portion to about two feet off the water. With a little help from Mitchell and Calista down below, he was able to swing one of his bare legs up and over the side. Once that leverage was gained, he was able to pull himself up and into the raft. Inside, he turned and looked down at the kids in the water below. Bracing himself on the edge of the raft, he reached a strong hand down to his niece. It was as if she were in a different world. She didn't seem to notice Dale talking to her.

"Come on Cally, take my hand."

Calista wasn't as gentle. She screamed at her cousin.

"Dammit Cally I'm gonna die, we're all going to die out here if you don't get up there. Come on! Don't wimp out on us now!"

Cally was bracing herself on the side of the raft. Hanging on to the raft was difficult in the huge seas. Hanging on to hope was even harder. She had lost it while drifting out there by herself for what seemed like an eternity. She had considered letting go of that line and just floating away to go see her Grandfather in heaven.  But Mitchell had rescued her and now Cally knew she needed to find the strength so that she could make his effort worthwhile.  She looked over at her family and noticed that they were yelling at her to get in the raft.  Without a word, Cally shimmied her way along the edge toward Dale who had positioned himself in front of the open tent flap.

"Grab my hand, climb up, swing your leg up here and Mitch will push you up from behind."

"OK Dale I'll try, I'm full of water though."

Water had filled Cally's survival suit and she was carrying perhaps an extra 40 or 50 pounds along with her 5'10" frame as she tried to climb into the raft. With no footholds to be found for leverage, she tried to swing her leg up while holding onto Dale's hand. Mitch pushed from behind with everything he had. The effort failed though and Cally went plunging back into the water.

"Come on try again Cally.  You can do it.  You can do it."  Calista gently nudged Cally back toward the raft. "Get up there."

Growing more determined, Cally took a stroke in the water to reposition herself next to the raft for another attempt to climb in.  This time Mitchell wedged himself underneath his cousin and reached up for a handhold on the raft above to use for leverage. Meanwhile, Dale widened his base and reached down and took her hand. Everyone helped. Everyone encouraged in their own way.

Cally was in a state of exhaustion, atrabiliousness, and confusion. But with the help of her family, she struggled up the side of the life raft. Finally, she was able to secure one leg up on the pontoon to her right. That was enough for Dale to grab her with both hands and drag her over the edge and into the interior of the raft. As she fell into the raft, the water that had filled her suit emptied onto the floor inside.

Laying face first in the raft, Cally rolled to get her head and mouth out of the pool of sea water that covered the surface of the raft floor. She scooted to the back edge of the raft. She knew that Mitchell and Calista would be coming through the flap soon and she wanted to get as far away from that as she could; which, of course, wasn't very far. She looked toward Dale at the opening of the canopy. His back was to her and he was looking down below. She heard voices and knew that they were talking to each other, but she was numb to the severity of their circumstances. She was in very bad shape.

Cally knew she should help get Mitchell and Calista in the raft, but she couldn't move. She just lay there and stared, trying to calm herself. This was hard because she was terrified. She had stared death in the face in that ocean and she was still alive. As she looked at Dale helping Mitchell into the raft Cally thought that they were going to die, only now it was going to be a slow death instead of a quick one. She was overwhelmed with dread, threatening to become hysterical.

Mitchell could hear Cally sobbing as his dad's strong hand helped him up and over the edge of the raft. He looked around in the dark. The raft was small. He didn't see how they were all going to fit in there. Cally was already taking up half of it as she lay across the center, crying incoherently. She didn't even notice when he told her to stop. Mitchell was stoic throughout. He felt like crying too. He was as scared as any of them, but crying wasn't in the Pruitt job description. No crying here. Besides, there was work to be done. This wasn't turning out to be the trip he had anticipated all year long. The very first fishing trip to crew with his dad, to really crew, and the boat was headed to the bottom of the ocean. Reality began to set in. He yelled at his sobbing cousin.

"Cally! Shut up! That is not helping."

The sharp rebuke worked momentarily and she stopped, though she seemed not to notice that anyone else was with her in the raft. As it was, three fourths of the crew was up and out of the water and Calista was on her way up as well.

She needed no help getting in. The youngest, smallest and most agile crewmember scrambled up the side and into the raft with ease. Inside the tent-like canopy there was very little room. It was rectangular in shape; perhaps six feet by four. She made her way inside to where Mitchell and Cally both lay. Cally was still sobbing fitfully. Calista climbed over legs to get herself to an open spot on the far end of the raft.

Dale was still sitting at the flap-like entrance of the raft peering outside. In the dark, cold storm he could see the silhouette of the *F/V Magnum's* hull bobbing in the waves 100 feet away. The raft was still tethered to the foundering boat. While the taut line provided some stability for them against the raging sea, Dale knew that it could mean trouble. He turned toward the inside of the raft, closed the flap to the outside and assessed the situation.

The first order of business was to inventory the emergency equipment onboard. The second was to find a way to get warm. He tried to take control of the situation, but he was disoriented and exhausted. Adrenaline had kept him alive in the water. Now that he was out, he was in pain and having difficulty thinking straight.

Calista stepped up as the vocal leader in the raft. She tried to get Cally to calm down. Mitchell was mellow, but Cally was still in a state of hysteria. Dale was showing signs of hypothermia. He was shaking and numb. The bottom of the raft was covered with frigid sea water from Cally's survival suit. There was no place for Dale in the raft without being in water; finally he just plopped down in it. Body heat eventually warmed the sitting water a bit. They'd have to bail it out soon. However, first they needed to search for emergency equipment on board the raft.

The four struggled to get their bodies into a tolerable position in the raft. Initially, Dale and Mitchell lay on one side. Cally and Calista claimed the other. As they were struggling to get comfortable, Calista found a blue emergency bag. She immediately began to look through it. In the bag were two bottle openers, two things that looked to them like cheap plastic space suits (actually called Thermal Protective Aids or TPAs), some foam insulation, a few flares, a bailer bucket, a sponge, a small first aid kit, a sea anchor, two oars, rusted batteries, a flashlight, a broken extra bulb, two packs of fishing line, dull scissors and a mirror.

Calista was thrilled at the find, but when she looked up she saw Cally shivering violently. Mitchell was absently staring into the distance and her dad's eyes riveted blankly on her.

Calista's family was in bad shape suffering in the weather, but oddly enough she had begun to feel much better. The sea sickness was gone. She felt alert and energized. She was scared, but she managed to push the fear to the back of her mind because there was work to do. She asked if everyone was okay. Cally said her head hurt. She thought she hit it on the deck winch when she fell into the water.

She rubbed the sore spot on her head where it hurt while she said this. Mitchell and Dale said they were fine. Calista wasn't so sure about her dad. She thought that maybe he got hit by some of those tools flying around the wheelhouse when the boat was going down. She knew that Dale was bordering on hypothermia from the cold water. She figured she'd probably switch sides in the raft if they were in there for very long so that she could be on Dad's side and take care of him.

Calista pulled a pair of rusty scissors from the emergency pack.

"Dad, when that piece of junk goes down, it's going to take us down with it. I'm going to cut the rope with these scissors."

"Don't pop the raft with those things." Mitchell was paying attention after all.

"I don't know Calista; if we cut the line we can't get back to the boat." Dale mumbled.

"Dad there is no way I'm getting back in that water. I think we should cut the line. It's gonna take us down when it sinks."

"Well I'm pretty sure these rafts are designed to release themselves from the boat if it starts sinking. The line will be cut when it goes down."

"Dad, do you want to rely on this piece of junk working right? Nothing on this boat has worked right. I'm gonna cut it."

Dale was in no condition to argue. He felt weak and cold and his fifteen year old daughter, the one who had been sick and whining for the entire trip, was taking over the operation. Dale was glad for this. As much as he wanted to be in charge and save the family, he knew at this point that they needed each other. If that meant letting Calista call some of the shots then so be it. She's a sharp kid, he thought. Tough. Calista Marie Pruitt was not your average fifteen year old girl.

Calista took the scissors, poked her head through the flap and outside into the storm. The few minutes that they had been inside with the flap closed had warmed the interior a bit. She felt the cold and driving sea spray hit her as she grabbed the line that fastened to the *Magnum*.

She looked over at the silhouette of the exposed hull and pondered for a moment. How did this happen? Her dad is the best. He'd been here a thousand times; and the one trip she goes on, the boat capsizes. It all seemed like a nightmare. But the cold water pelting her face made her pretty sure that it was real. She started in on the line. The scissors were dull and she thought that they wouldn't even be able to cut paper. But she sawed away on the thick line anyway. She had no luck trying to cut through the line itself so she took to cutting the thin individual braids of rope that were woven together. After several minutes of cutting, Calista gave up the effort. There was no way to cut the sea painter with those scissors.

"Dad I can't cut it."

"Come back inside, Calista. We'll have to take our chances that the line will release if it goes down. Come back in and close that flap."

Calista came back inside and closed the flap. They quickly learned that having the flap closed was a good thing. The warmth and shelter provided by the canopy were welcomed. Calista came inside and took her place alongside a whimpering, shivering Cally. They looked at each other, but said nothing. The crew gradually began to calm down. Dale and Mitchell were quiet on the other side of the raft. Finally Calista broke the silence.

"Dad put this space suit thing on. I think it's supposed to help keep you warm."

Lethargic, Dale didn't respond.

"Dad!" She yelled. He slowly turned toward her. His eyes were glazed. He was shivering uncontrollably.

"What?"

"You need to put this on." She had the TPA out of its plastic container and held it up. Mitchell chimed in from his position next to Dale.

"Yeah, Dad, we have to get you warmed up. If you go into a coma we're all dead. Come on, put it on."

Mitchell had just finished a marine safety course at Kodiak High School called AMSEA. His teacher, Jane Eisemann, had taught the class about severity of hypothermia. Mitchell knew that something had to be done quickly to warm dad.

Calista leaned over Cally and pushed her over to the outside. She climbed over her cousin; Cally was now on the outside and Calista held an inside spot. She was next to Dale while Mitchell was on the other outside spot. The raft's size dictated that any movement by one person required the movement of someone else to create space.

On either side of their dad, Calista and Mitchell tried to work him into the thin, clear plastic body suit. It seemed to be made of the type of plastic used to cover a new DVD. They didn't think it would really create the warmth he needed. But in desperation they had to try something. Dale helped them as best as he could when they tried to get his legs in. Once his legs were inside, he raised up his behind so they could work the suit up and over his body. As they did this, holes ripped in the plastic suit. But they managed to get it over his body and stuff his arms in as well. Unfortunately, by the time they finished, the TPA had ripped badly. Dale's every movement caused the TPA to rip a bit more. Finally, in frustration he tore the remaining pieces off of his body. Angrily he yelled, "This thing's a piece of junk!"

"Uncle Dale, what's going to happen?"

"We're going to get rescued, that's what's gonna happen."

"How are they going to know where we are?"

Well I got a Mayday out and the EPIRB (emergency position-indicating radio beacons) should be going off. There's probably a Coast Guard plane or a fishing boat on their way right now. We'll just have to sit tight and wait."

"Dad we have to get this water out of here. You can't sit in that too long. Calista, give me that bucket."

Calista gave Mitchell the bucket and then opened the flap a little. Mitchell started bailing. It was difficult because the water pooled around Dale because he was the heaviest person in the life raft. Adding to the problem of the water in the raft was that waves from the storm outside came in when the flap was open.

Calista began opening and closing the flap when Mitchell was ready to throw some water overboard. They soon realized that this wasn't working. They couldn't get enough water into the bucket. When they threw it out, bucket spillage, combined with new water coming in, made the endeavor pointless. Casting around for something to help, Calista remembered the sponge that she saw in the emergency bag.

"Mitchell! We can use the sponge!"

Taking turns, Mitchell and Calista spent the next half hour sopping up sponge loads of water out of the bottom of the raft and squeezing the water into the ocean. They kept heat in the raft since they were able to reach a hand under a smaller opening in the flap and squeeze the water outside. The sponge worked! The crew was able to eliminate most of the water that they had been sitting in. Sitting in the water had not been much of a problem for anybody but Dale since the kids all had survival suits on. They knew that the first step toward protecting their dad was done. He was no longer sitting in cold water.

The crew lay down in four rows like sardines. It was quiet for some time. All four were wondering how this had happened. Dale apologized over and over.

"It's not your fault Dad. We can't worry about that right now. We have to get you warm. Mrs. Eisemann said that you lose 80% of your heat through your head," observed Mitchell, remembering his course. "We need to make dad a hat."

Calista once again picked through the emergency pack. She pulled out a large piece of foam that looked as if it had been used for packing the kit.

"Dad we can wrap this around your head; that should help," she said.

She held up the piece of foam. It was dark and hard to see. Dale was only half listening anyway.

From either side of their dad, Calista and Mitchell began working on a hat. They wrapped the piece of foam around his head and while Mitchell held the foam in place, Calista ripped off a long piece of the space suit that he had torn earlier. She took that strip and wrapped it around the foam like a headband securing the foam to his head. The makeshift hat helped a little. It would have to do since there was nothing else in the raft that could help keep his body warm.

# CHAPTER EIGHT

At approximately 1:00 A.M. on Thursday, June 21st, the crew had been in the raft for two hours. They had periodically peeked under the flap to see the dark silhouette of the *Magnum's* hull as it bobbed in the Shelikof Strait. It had not yet sunk, but they were still attached to it. Too much time had passed. Dale was beginning to think that his mayday had not been heard by anybody; nor had the EPIRB beacon functioned properly.

The Coast Guard Air Station in Kodiak is one of the largest Coast Guard bases in the United States. HH-65 Dolphins and HH-60 Jayhawk helicopters, along with HC-130 fixed-wing aircraft are stationed there and on call for immediate departure. Any of these aircraft could reach their location from the Kodiak base in minutes. If the mayday had been heard, or if the EPIRB had emitted its emergency signal, they'd have been found by now. He had given their location in the mayday. *Two miles off of Unalishagvak.* Locating them wouldn't be a problem. They had the flares at the ready and their ears strained for planes overhead, but they heard nothing.

"I don't think they're coming."

"What do you mean Dad? You got a mayday off and so did I."

In the skiff, Calista had grabbed the VHF skiff radio and yelled mayday into it just as they had to abandon ship. She had dropped the radio and wished now that she hadn't.

"They'd be here by now. It only takes 'em about twenty or thirty minutes to get over here. Nobody heard it."

"They could still be coming." It was Cally. She had calmed down and had been mostly quiet and withdrawn.

"They're not coming and if we don't get some rain water we may not make it."

"Dad don't talk that way! What are you doing?"

"I know Calista, you're right. I'm just saying that I don't think anybody heard us which means no one will know we're down."

"Mom will. She'll be worried when we don't show."

"Yeah, in ten hours she will be. We need to be ready to be out here a while; to do that we need water. We can stick the bailer out there when it starts to rain and collect water."

"Oh my God, Uncle Dale."

Cally's voice trailed off. Calista couldn't see Cally on the other side of their dark living compartment, but she knew she was suffering.

"We're going to be OK, Cally," Calista said reassuringly. "They'll find us."

Calista opened the corner of the flap one more time and peered out at the hull in the black ocean. The waves were huge. She wondered why she wasn't sick anymore. How strange, she thought, that she had been so sick on that big boat when the weather wasn't all that bad. Now, major seas and high winds were tossing this tiny raft around and she wasn't sick at all. The shadowy hull of the *Magnum* looked smaller. It seemed to be gradually sinking. She wondered why it wasn't sinking faster; she decided to try and cut the rope again. Dale had already explained to her that the hydro release was designed to detach the sea painter if the vessel sank, but Calista didn't trust it. She decided that she didn't trust anything having to do with that boat. She grabbed the flashlight and turned it on. Nothing; it was dead.

"Oh great!" wailed Calista. "Flashlight's dead. This is just perfect. The extra batteries are rusted, the extra bulb's broken and here we are, sitting in the dark!"

There was no reply.

"Are you guys awake? We need to stay focused."

Calista checked to see that her family was awake. Everybody was, although she thought that she had awakened Dale when she asked him.

"We need to stay awake. No sleeping or we'll die of hypothermia."

"Ok Calista, we'll stay awake," Dale replied sleepily.

"She's right Dad. Especially you. You're the one that's gonna die if we can't get you warm or get some help or something."

"I'm fine Mitchell. I just wish I hadn't put you guys in this situation."

"Dad, help me find the scissors." Calista changed the subject.

"Well where did you put them Calista?"

"I don't know Dad, I don't remember. I thought they'd be in the bag, But I just felt around in there and couldn't find them."

"Well feel around everyone. Those things could pop this raft."

Everyone set to feeling around their area for the scissors that Calista had been using to try to cut the line. No luck.

"Geez, Calista, this is not good."

"Dad, they're not gonna pop the raft. These things couldn't cut a piece of paper! I want to work on cutting that line before that boat pulls us all down to the bottom of the stupid ocean!"

"Calista relax. If the boat sinks, the line will release and we'll drift around until the Coast Guard comes and gets us. We've got to think positively. No more negativity. Understood?"

Deep down Dale was badly worried about the hydro release. He knew that boats sometimes take time to sink and when they do they don't always descend directly to the bottom. Depending on the amount of trapped air inside, a sinking boat can float around at different levels under water for quite some time.

Dale thought about the *F/V Horizon*, a fishing boat that sunk near the southeast coast of Kodiak Island in January of 2006. The crew was rescued by another fishing boat in the fleet. One week later the boat was found beached miles away from where it had sunk. It hadn't sunk clear down to the ocean floor. Instead, it had drifted around under the ocean surface.

Dale figured that the *Magnum* was getting ready to go down. He hoped and prayed that the hydro release would work as designed. If it did go down and the hydro release didn't cut the line, they still might survive if the boat floated below the surface for awhile. They had 100 feet of leeway which is the length of the *Sea Painter*. Whatever the case, he couldn't dwell on it. He couldn't show panic. He had to hide his fear from the kids. That's what skippers do.

"We don't have to worry about that line. The scissors must have fallen overboard since they're not in here. Even if they are, they're so dull that they wouldn't pop this raft or cut the line. So quit looking for them. What we need to do is relax, save our energy, and wait for them to come get us. The EPIRB is going off and the Coast Guard will be here soon to rescue us. Sometimes with EPIRBs they're a little slower because they go off by accident. They have to make sure it's really an emergency. They probably have been trying to get us up on the radio since we haven't been answering. They're getting ready to come find us. The thing we need to do is stay calm and stay positive."

"And stay warm. I'm freezing," Cally chimed in.

Calista almost fired off a sarcastic retort to Cally's comment. Something about feeling sorry for yourself for being cold when Dale's lying there with nothing on; but she took her dad's words to heart and stayed positive.

"Snuggle up to Mitchell over there Cally. That'll warm you up."

Mitchell didn't complain when his cousin scooted closer and put an arm around him. It was cold in the raft, but the heat of their bodies made it bearable as long as they were able to keep the flap closed.

At 2:00 A.M. on Island Lake, Mindy lay awake in the master bedroom on their king-sized bed. Their home is in a remote area. They have four or five neighbors on their side of the lake and several on the other side. They love their rural way of life where everyone is known and anyone is welcome.

This is the type of place where people don't lock their doors. Not only do the Pruitts not lock the doors to their cars, they don't even remove the keys. It is deathly quiet on Island Lake at 2:00 A.M. The only thing to break the silence is a loon or the occasional Kodiak Grizzly Bear making its way up Pruitt Lane.

This night was no different. Total silence, but Mindy was used to that. She had spent her share of nights lying awake in this bed listening to the silence. It seemed to be the one time in her life when she could get some peace and quiet. Their life was good and she wouldn't change it for the world. But making a go of commercial fishing had been a challenge to say the least.

Fluctuating prices, government regulations, time spent apart, and big bills take their toll on a family. The industry consistently ranks as the most dangerous job in the world. In 2005, fisherman died at a rate of 118 per 100,000, easily outdistancing second-place logging as the most likely job to kill a person.

Being the wife of a commercial fisherman is not easy. Running the business, being a single mom for most of the year, and the loneliness that can come from months on end without her husband had caused Mindy much stress over the years. But Mindy Pruitt was tough. Her life was hectic and she relished the middle-of-the-night quiet on Island Lake.

She didn't like this kind of quiet however. It seemed somehow ominous. She was happy that it would be ending tomorrow, but she still felt faintly uneasy. She should have been feeling pure joy because her babies were coming home and her man too. But she didn't. She couldn't relax and she couldn't sleep. She hoped Calista's kidney problems were OK. She reminded herself over and over that by this time tomorrow, the whole family would be asleep in the house. Finally her tired body won out. She fell asleep.

"Stay low! Stay low! Don't' get up for any reason! Lay back and stay low!"

"Dad what's going on?"

The crew members inside the raft were suddenly being tossed about as if inside a washing machine. Dale was yelling instructions. A wave had very nearly capsized the raft. Until now the life raft had been somewhat stable despite the intensity of the storm that had blown up. But suddenly they were up against tremendous seas and were in immediate danger of flipping over. Dale knew that he didn't have to tell the kids what would happen if they went over right now, but his fear made him repeat himself.

"Lay flat and stay low! The boat must have sunk. We're drifting free now."

"Oh my God! Oh my God!" Cally exclaimed.

"Cally, calm down. Just lay flat and we should be OK."

"Dad, should I look to see if the boat's out there?"

"No! No! Just lay flat."

Another huge wave nearly flipped the raft over. Panicked screams filled the compartment as the craft recovered.

"Oh my God, Uncle Dale!"

This time he didn't respond. Without getting up, Dale reached behind his head to make sure the flap was securely fastened. He knew they couldn't afford to take on much water. The flap was in place and seemed to be holding. Again, he told everyone to lie down and be calm. Fear filled his chest, but he remained resolute.

He kept talking to his frightened crew, reminding them over and over to lay flat and calm themselves.

The craft had finally broken free from the capsized *F/V Magnum*. The tired old vessel sank in the Shelikof Strait. The Hydro Release had worked as designed. The stability that the capsized hull of the *F/V Magnum* had lent to the life raft was gone. The four crew members in the tiny raft were now at the mercy of the seething, pitching storm of the mighty Shelikof Strait. The Pruitts are not an especially church-going family, but for the next several hours every person in that raft was praying to God.

At six A.M. Mindy finally got out of bed. She didn't think she had slept much, but she felt energized. Today was the day! She went downstairs to the kitchen and brewed a pot of coffee. She looked out at the lake from her kitchen window. The banya, which stood on the shores of the lake, had a sprinkling of frost on the roof. A banya is a wood-heated sauna. They can be found throughout the island, a local tradition.

This banya was a replacement for the first one which had burned down in a fire of unknown origin.

A rectangular wooden building, approximately sixteen feet by ten feet, it contains two small rooms inside. You enter the banya into a changing and sitting room. A wall separates it into two sections. A door in that wall leads from the sitting room to the sauna room. Benches run along two walls. In the opposite corner is a large iron wood stove. Sitting atop the wood stove is a giant iron pot of water. There's a drain in the middle and a water hose near the benches. Light a fire in the stove, wait an hour or so, and you've got a comfortable and relaxing wet sauna.

It brought a smile to Mindy's face that morning, thinking of how the boys would be sitting in the banya later on in the day. She and Calista might even have their time as well if she could manage it. They might need to wait a day or two for that.

The Pruitts enjoy their banyas steaming hot and nude, so typically they are gender specific. Mindy wasn't too concerned whether she and Calista would relax in the banya that night. She was coming home. That was all that mattered. Her quiet home would turn into family bedlam. That made her smile.

Mindy poured a second cup, went back up the stairs, showered, and got ready for work. She would put in a couple of hours, return home, and get ready for their homecoming. She had to go to the store, clean the bathroom, take the truck to the dock, and, oh yes, the ferns. She had forgotten that her friend Robinette was coming to dig up some of her ferns. It was going to be a busy day; a wonderfully busy day.

# CHAPTER NINE

The seas had subsided somewhat by daybreak. The crew inside of the life raft was physically and mentally drained from the chaos. The winds had dropped from a ferocious 40-50 miles per hour to a just bearable 20-30. Such winds were normal for the Shelikof Strait. The Strait is 130 miles long and 30 miles wide. It has dramatic and unstable tide changes along with strong currents. Alaska State Ferry boats, an occasional tanker, and the few hardy commercial fishermen are the only ship traffic in this part of the world. A six by eight-foot life raft could bob around in these seas for months without being spotted by another human. Dale knew from long experience on these waters that the northwest wind had blown them south into the middle of the

Strait somewhere. They were on their own somewhere in the Shelikof.

Mitchell opened the flap to peer outside; nothing out there but ocean. It was the first time the flap had been opened since the raft had broken free from the *Magnum.* They felt the temperature drop instantly inside the canopy.

"Mitchell, close that thing. It's cold out there." Cally's voice was subdued now. The panic was gone; replaced by melancholy. Mitchell closed the flap.

The crew lay in the raft side by side and listened. They listened to the tent flap in the wind.

"Was that a plane? I think I heard a plane," someone muttered.

Dale felt like he had to do something. "I'm going to shoot a flare. Maybe someone is looking for us nearby."

Really he thought that nobody was looking for them. He knew that if the EPIRB was signaling, or if someone had heard his mayday they'd have already been on the scene. They had been in the life raft for seven or eight hours already and hadn't heard a boat, plane, or helicopter. But now Calista (or was it Cally he didn't know) said she heard a plane. Dale readied the flare gun with one of the flares and opened the flap. Cold wind whipped into their living space as he did so. He climbed up, sat on the edge of the raft, and shot a flare into the sky. Its red streak shot into the clouds and then disappeared. Nothing. He looked around, hoping. Could someone out there have seen it? He knew it was false hope and that there was no one out there to see it. No rescue effort was underway. If they knew the Pruitts were down, they'd be out in full force. They'd be hearing planes and helicopters flying everywhere.

The thought caused a sinking feeling in Dale's stomach. Nobody knew they were in distress; not the fleet, not the Coast Guard, not even Mindy. He thought of his call to Clint. He must not have called Dale back to check on him. Not surprisingly. Fishermen get busy and don't always follow through. Dale didn't blame Clint, though he wished he had called back. Had he done so, he would have known something was wrong when Dale didn't answer up. Nobody knew; nobody would know for hours still.

Dale did not share these thoughts with the kids. Earlier he had mandated that everyone stay positive. He would continue to follow that rule. The last thing he needed was for them to panic or lose hope. He looked out once more and then climbed back in and closed the flap. It was going to be a long day.

"Nobody saw that one. I think maybe I should have saved it."

"We have more Dad. We'll just keep listening for planes and fire one off when we hear one."

"Yep, yep. That's what we'll do. Someone should be along soon." Dale's white lie seemed to comfort his crew.

Mindy pulled her Chevy pickup into the parking lot of the Family Center. A basketball court for the kids was right outside of the facility she helped to build. Three young Alutiiq boys were playing tag inside the fenced basketball area. The game stopped briefly for the three to yell, "Hi Miss Mindy".

"Hi boys. How are your folks?"

"Fine."

"Tell them hi for me."

"O.K. Bye Miss Mindy."

"Bye boys. You have a good day."

"O.K."

Game on. The boys immediately began laughing and chasing each other around the court. Mindy walked into the building.

"Yo!" The greeting came from behind the computer in the office adjacent to the main Family Center game room that Mindy had entered.

"Hey Mister Nick, how are ya? Didja tear it up last night?"

"Nah, home and in bed by ten. Family home yet?" replied her co-worker without looking up from his computer. Nick was Mindy's 'partner in crime' at the Family Center. He and Mindy had a wonderful working relationship.

"You know Nick they're gonna be home this afternoon. I'm just here finishing up some paperwork and then I'm going to be gone by ten or so. You can handle things can't you?"

"Oh sure, you can count on me. I'll pick the kiddos up this afternoon and cover all of your other duties as well, like usual!"

"You're the best Nick. That's why I love ya. You'll always do all my dirty work for me."

Mindy made her way into her office and settled in for a few hours of work. She had been there for about fifteen minutes when her cell phone rang; she saw on the digital readout that it was Robinette.

"Hey kiddo how are ya?"

"Great Min! I'm on my way to work and just need to know one thing."

"OK, what's that?"

"Red or white?"

"Why red of course dear! What time are you coming by?"

"I was thinking about four. How does that sound?"

"That sounds great. Dale and the kiddos should be home by then."

"Wanna reschedule? Have a little family time?"

"Don't be ridiculous dear. You're as much family as the rest of 'em."

"OK, well if Dale's gonna be home maybe I'll bring two bottles."

"Oh the old man'll be fine. He has some gin in the cupboard. I'm sure he'd rather have that anyway."

"Sounds good Min. Hey! Gotta run! See you tonight."

"OK, Robinette. Thanks for the shout."

Mindy hung up the phone and went back to work. Another hour or so and she'd be outta there.

Minutes on the raft crawled by. The hours dragged. They were doing their best to stay awake though they wondered why. If they slept, at least the time would go faster. Mitchell had talked about the need to keep Dale awake. He was still shivering and his skin looked pasty. He was not doing so well. The kids knew that they needed to keep a close eye on him. Calista had been spending a lot of time draped over his body trying to keep him warm. She was talking to him constantly.

Sometimes he ignored her and other times he would talk to her. Calista tried to lighten the mood to keep the crew's spirits up.

"Let's sing."

"Sing yourself Calista." She was happy that she at least got Mitchell to respond. He had been pretty quiet; staring absently at the opposite wall of the canopy.

"No really, let's sing. Come on". She broke into *Itty Bitty* by Alan Jackson.

*Have a little love on a little honeymoon*
*You got a little dish and you got a little spoon*
*An itty bitty house and an itty bitty yard*
*Itty bitty dog and an itty bitty car*

*Well, it's alright to be itty bitty*
*Little hometown or a big old city*
*Might as well share, might as well smile*
*Life goes on for an itty bitty while*

By the second chorus, Cally had joined in and they finished the song word for word. Dale and Mitchell didn't join in, but they didn't complain; anything to break the monotony. They were both grateful for Calista's spirit. Mitchell couldn't believe how spunky she was now after all her fussing while they were still fishing. The *Itty Bitty* song reminded them all of Grandpa Pruitt who used to dance with the grandkids to that song at family gatherings. The singing brought a welcome relief to their very grim situation.

When they finished the song, Calista broke into Taylor Swift's *Picture to Burn*. Cally joined in on this one too, but with less fervor. *Itty Bitty* was part of her psyche with the history she had with her Grandfather. This song she liked, but she was losing interest. Calista sang a couple more Taylor Swift songs by herself and the rest of the crew listened intently. It helped to pass the time. Calista began to sing *Itty Bitty* a second time when she noticed that Dale was sleeping next to her. He looked dead. His skin was white and puffy and it scared her.

"Dad." She whispered and shook him gently and he came to and looked over at her. His eyes were bloodshot and tired. He stared blankly at her for a moment.

"Sounds good Sweetheart, are you going to sing some more?"

"Sure Dad. She broke into *Itty Bitty* again."

Mindy left the Family Center about 11:00 on Thursday morning. On her way home she stopped at the Safeway to pick up apple juice, cranberry/pomegranate juice, and other things she knew that Calista, Mitchell, and Dale would like to eat when they got home. Arriving at the house on Pruitt Lane, she had a quick lunch and began to put the house in order. Dale always appreciated the preparations she made for his return from the sea.

A clean house and his favorite meal after a long fishing trip was part of the job's allure. This trip was different for Mindy. Usually, Calista and Mitchell were busy helping her get ready for Dale's return. Now Mindy was alone. She busied herself with the housekeeping chores. She even went outside to split some wood and get the stove in the banya ready. She worked hard all afternoon. Robinette would be coming soon and she could relax then with her friend and a good glass of red.

On the raft, the boredom was a constant, mind-numbing fact. The winds were still blowing wildly, but the crew had gained some confidence in the seaworthiness of their little vessel. They'd risen over 10 to 15 foot crests and rode down into the deep troughs behind those crests for about 20 hours. The initial shock and fear had somewhat subsided. They now knew that if they laid low in the raft, it could handle the waves they were encountering.

As they passed a full day in the life raft, their greatest concern began to be the lack of fresh drinking water. They were thirsty. The emergency pack had no water. Dale knew it was a looming emergency. Frustration was mounting and the crew was getting cranky.

"Dad it's rained every day of my life in Kodiak. Why won't it rain?"

"I don't know Mitch."

Kodiak gets an average of 76 inches of precipitation annually. But the winds the crew had been contending with did not bring rain.

Mitchell thought about his AMSEA class in Mrs. Eisenmann's room. He remembered her talking about how men in survival situations at sea were often tempted to drink the sea water because their thirst was so intense. Mitchell was tempted himself, but he knew better. He knew from class that it would only serve to dehydrate and kill you quicker. He wouldn't be drinking any water from the ocean. He felt like they'd be rescued soon anyway. He could wait. His thoughts drifted to his girlfriend Candice back in Kodiak. He sure did miss her. He also thought fondly of his mother. He wasn't sure what time it was, but he figured it was probably past the time they were supposed to be home.

"Mom will be freaking out soon." He wasn't sure if he said it or just thought it until Calista replied.

"She probably already is. I'm sure she's called the Coast Guard already and they're out looking for us."

"Uncle Dale do you think the Coast Guard is looking for us?"

No reply.

"Uncle Dale?"

Calista had been lying back in the raft and staring up at the ceiling. She had taken her eyes off her dad for how many minutes? She didn't know. But now she rolled and propped herself up on elbows to see that Dale was asleep again. His face and neck were bloated and white.

"Dad.' She gave a gentle shake like the time before only this time he didn't come to. Immediate panic filled her and she shook his shoulder.

"Dad! Wake up!" she screamed.

This time Dale came to and looked over at her with bleary eyes.

"Dad quit doing that!"

"I was just taking a nap Calista." His voice was soft and drained.

"Dad you didn't wake up the first time I tried. Stop doing that."

"Is that a plane?" Mitchell interrupted.

The crew immediately perked up and began listening intently. Wind battered the side of the raft. The flapping of the vessel's canopy portion made it hard to hear anything. Calista also kept on talking which caused the rest of the crew to yell at her to shut up. They couldn't tell if they had heard a boat or a plane or nothing. They discussed shooting another flare, but Dale nixed the idea.

"We need to be sure something's out before we shoot another one. I wasted that other one I don't want to do that again."

# CHAPTER TEN

Mindy was unloading the dishwasher in the kitchen when Robinette walked in the front door and began removing her shoes. No need for her to knock; that wouldn't be the Pruitt way. Leaving the machine half filled with clean dishes, Mindy dried her hands with a dish towel and gave her friend a big hug. They exchanged the small talk of old friends. Mindy asked how Robinette's dad was.

"Fine", she said as she pulled two bottles of wine (one red and one white) out of her grocery bag.

"Couldn't remember what you said this morning."

"Better safe than sorry, huh Robinette?"

"You know it. No family yet?" Robinette nodded toward the empty house.

"No, not yet; probably down offloading the fish." Mindy went back to work on the unfinished dishwasher. "Let me finish this up right quick and we'll get started."

"When were you expecting them in?" Robinette inquired.

"Oh shoulda been in 'bout early afternoon," Mindy replied as she continued with her task. "Probably decided to keep fishing or they're busy offloading and he hasn't had the chance to call yet. No worries, Robinette. Now go on and open up that bottle of red. I said red this morning. Let's go get some tools."

Mindy gave a wink as she whisked by her, walked to the entryway and sat down to put on her boots. Robinette opened the bottle, grabbed a couple of glasses, and followed her friend out the front door.

Pruitt Lane is only a few feet from the front door of their home. Robinette looked across the one-lane dirt road at the single pole with the basketball hoop Dale had put up years ago. Robinette shuddered slightly at the sight of the empty hoop. She was surprised at Mindy's nonchalance about Dale and the kids. By Robinette's measure, they were already a few hours late. (It was true that time estimates in the salmon fishing industry were very elastic.)

But still, they were late. Dale should have called. Robinette didn't have much time to think about this as Mindy was already digging up ferns from the side of the house for Robinette to take home. Robinette wasn't about to add any negative vibes to the situation. Grabbing the shovel Mindy handed her, she pushed down her concerns about the crew being late.

Mitchell poked his head out of a small opening in the flap and saw that it was getting dark. It was foggy and windy, but not raining. He figured they were pushing 24 hours without so much as a hint of a rescue.

"We are so screwed. Dad, why won't it rain?"

"I don't know Mitch."

They had discovered that the raft came equipped with a built-in water catch. It fed rainwater from the roof above into a pocket leading to a spigot inside; all well and good if Mother Nature was cooperating. Unfortunately for the Pruitts, she wasn't.

They had endured high seas for a full day and night without water. The usually wet skies were not cooperating and the crew suffered.

Heading into their second night aboard the tiny life raft had turned their mood to despair. They had shifted spots several times throughout the day once the seas had settled. Each had taken turns unzipping the flap and peering outside. No one had seen anything except ocean and fog. These brief periods of activity were separated by hours of nothing. No sound, no talking. Nothing but staying low in the raft and shifting to keep the legs busy.

There was some sporadic conversation from time to time, but it never lasted long. It mostly involved complaining about the terrible situation they were in.

Calista kept a close watch on her father throughout the day. She occasionally shifted and looked out the flap, but was insistent that she be 'next to Dad'. The two of them did the most talking in the raft that day. But as nightfall began and she felt like she needed to take a nap, she made Cally and Mitch promise to keep a close eye on him.

"Watch Dad you guys, I have to sleep."

"OK Calista, we'll watch him." Mitchell replied, dismissively.

"No, I'm serious Mitch. Half the time I'm not sure if you're awake over there."

Calista and Mitchell were on opposite sides of the raft. Both were lying on their backs, staring at the ceiling. Neither could see the other. There was no other sound in the raft. Mitchell wasn't sure if Cally (who was next to him) or his dad were awake. The oncoming darkness made it difficult to see the others.

"Well, Calista we can't stay awake forever. We need to sleep sometime."

"No kiddin'. That's what I plan to do." Her voice trailed off sleepily. "But you gotta watch Dad; you and Cally. Cally, you awake?"

Calista finally fell asleep. Mitchell's stared directly up into the darkness above. Again his mind drifted to thoughts of his girlfriend, Candice. He was all but dead, and she didn't yet have a clue. He turned his head.

"Dad, you awake?"

Mindy stood in front of the Pruitt home. She held two empty wine glasses in her hand and was leaning against Robinette's car. Robinette was in the driver's seat with the window open.

"Nicely done young lady."

"Why thank you. What now?"

"I'm going to head for home. Give me a call when he gets those kids in will ya?"

"Yeah, sure Rob. Thanks for the help. I'll call you."

Robinette noticed a change in her friend with that reply. She worried about her as she pulled the car out of the driveway and headed away from the house. She was amazed at what a cool customer Mindy was.

Mindy watched Robinette drive down the road. She walked into the house, took off her shoes, put the wine glasses in the machine, picked up the phone and dialed Calista's cell phone.

She left a message.

The crew of the *F/V Magnum* spent the night of Thursday, June 21st aboard the tiny inflatable raft drifting across the Shelikof Strait. In his lucid moments, Captain Dale had a pretty good idea of where they were. If only he had a radio, he could tell them where they were; tell them what happened. He felt terrible. He was in pain and so cold. He was responsible for the kids. He had to get them home. By this time he had grown even more confident in the sea worthiness of their tiny vessel. They had ridden out heaving seas the night before. Tonight the weather was much better; at least by Shelikof Strait standards.

Dale worried about the fresh-water situation as he lay on his back staring at the ceiling.

"We're gonna need some water soon." He said to no one in particular.

Nobody answered.

His thoughts turned to Mindy. He knew that by now, Mindy would begin to know that the boat was down.

She was about to discover for herself that Dale had not done his job. He had not brought her family home.

"I'm still trying, Min."

Dale wasn't sure if he whispered it, or if he just thought it. He did know that he wanted to yell to her. He figured they had drifted at least 10 or 15 miles, most likely to the southeast toward the southern tip of Kodiak Island. He wanted to open the flap and yell to his wife.

*Mindy! We're OK. The boat went down, but we made it to the life raft. She's sea worthy Mindy. We rode out a bitch of a storm last night in this thing. We'll ride it some more until they find us. Let them know we're out here. We're drifting near the southern tip of the island. But we're OK. We're going to be OK. The kids are doing fine Mindy.*

Dale listened to the wind and wave driven sound outside. Inside the tent, spray from the sea's waves hit the walls. The sound never changed. Dale wanted to pray. He wanted to read the Bible.

*They shoulda put some Bible verses in that emergency kit. Maybe laminate those things. Oh well, couldn't read them in here with a dead flashlight anyway.*

Captain Dale Pruitt lay alone with his thoughts. Everyone else in the raft was asleep.

*Beep............Hi you reached Calista Pruitt's cell phone. Leave a message. Bye!*

"Hi honey. It's me again. Where the heck are you guys? I'm still at home, so call me."

Mindy hung up the phone. It was the third message left for her daughter in the previous four hours. It was nearing Friday with no word from the fishermen. Mindy began pacing nervously from the kitchen through the dining room to the living room. She sat on the couch for 15 seconds before getting up and pacing back into the kitchen.

Where were they? She had made several attempts to call Dale on his cell phone as well. No answer.

She sat at the dining room table and talked to herself.

"They decided to keep fishing or they ducked into some cove with bad reception."

She went back into the kitchen and poured a glass of Merlot.

"This is not like Dale though. Why haven't you called, dammit?" She shouted.

That night Mindy cleaned some more. She thought of calling the Coast Guard right then, but decided that would be silly. How embarrassing it'd be to call them in missing when they're probably offloading fish at Ocean Beauty Seafood.

At first light on Friday, June 22nd Mindy Pruitt woke to the phone ringing.

"It's them!" She yelled as she dashed from the couch to the phone in the kitchen. She had finally slept for thirty minutes after a painful night of anxiety.

"Hello"

"Mindy, where's Dale with my fish?"

Mindy's heart sank. It was Cannery boss Tim Blott.

"Well Tim I don't know. I was planning to call you to ask the same question. You haven't heard from them either huh?"

"No"

"Well he must have ducked out of the weather to ride it out. It's sure not like him not to call though."

"He was supposed to offload at 4:00 in the afternoon yesterday. He should have called if he wasn't coming in. This sets us back over here Mindy."

"I know Tim, but you know he'd call.........he will call when he gets some reception. Weather looks better now, so I'm sure he'll be creeping out into the open any time now and he'll be able to ring us up."

"Well call me as soon as you hear from him will you? I have a busy day here and need to figure out when to get him."

Cannery boss Tim Blott had no way of knowing that his 10,000 pounds of Alaskan Salmon had been on the bottom of the Shelikof Strait for 30 hours.

"OK Tim. And you call me if you hear from him first. I'm going to kick his butt. Why didn't he call?"

Mindy hung up the phone and walked over to start the day's coffee. She made a full pot.

"I'm gonna need it." She said to herself.

She walked back over to the phone, picked it up, dialed Dale's cell phone. She left another message.

# CHAPTER ELEVEN

At 8:00 on Thursday morning, an Alaskan Marine Highway System ferry eased its way through the channel toward the Kodiak Ferry Terminal. James Pruitt was a passenger on the ferry. Standing at the rail next to his duffelled football gear, James looked up at graffiti written at the top of one of the stanchions supporting the Fred Zharoff Bridge. *Don't Leave Me Babe* was scrawled about ten feet from the top of the hundred-foot pillar looming high above the channel.

To see the graffiti made him feel good. It meant he was home. Soon he would be aboard the *Magnum* and fishing with Mitch and Dale. He wasn't sure when they'd be in to get him, but he knew it wouldn't be long. They'd been out since Monday and now it was Friday. He figured that with a couple of girls on board they wouldn't be out there much longer. Probably they probably were already home. It didn't matter when, James thought, he'd be ready when they were.

He was home from football camp. Camp had been fun, but not the same for James without Mitchell, Ben, and Michael. One year behind his best buddies, James was going to miss them this year.

Mitchell and Ben were scheduled for college in California in September. Michael Holden had graduated early and had already enlisted in the Coast Guard.

His father, Jeff Holden was a 20-year Coast Guard veteran. When he retired, he and his wife Shawn settled in Kodiak where he joined the Kodiak Police Department. He was beloved in the community and trusted and respected by this group of teenagers.

With their dads' coaching, the four boys helped to put Kodiak Bear Football on the map in Alaskan State high school sports. The previous year they'd made it to the small school championship game.

This year would be tough since they'd lost so much. James was confident they'd do well again since they had some returning talent, but it just wouldn't be the same without Mitchell, Ben, and Michael.

As the ferry docked at the terminal, James grabbed his gear and headed toward the gangplank. Once on shore, he jumped in a buddy's car and got a ride to his home next door to Dale and Mindy's place on Island Lake.

"Dad I think I see land!"

The exclamation jolted Dale awake. Shivering, he rolled his head and shoulders over in order to see out of the open flap. A faint, but certain, outline of mountains was off in the distance. He rolled the rest of the way over to his stomach and began to shimmy toward the opening. He opened the flap completely and sat near the edge of the raft. He looked really rough with beard stubble and the crazy hat on his head.

Blue sky peaked through the marine layer. For the first time in the whole ordeal, the sun was shining. The rays felt good as he sat half outside, half inside. He didn't stay long though because the crew wanted to look also.

"Dad, let me see."

"No, I'm next Mitchell!"

"Oh my God, Calista!" Cally interjected, "are we in third grade?"

Dale moved out of the way and the jockeying began for a peak at the sweet sight of land.

"It's Red River. It's Kodiak, guys!"

"Oh my God, Oh my God! Uncle Dale we're going to make it!"

"Relax Cally. That's gotta be five, six miles away. But if we can get over there, there's a Fish and Game hunting cabin up there. We can climb up there and use the radio. Those places all have radios."

"Dad, let's paddle."

"The paddles are right here," said Mitchell, "they've been poking me in the back for about fifty hours."

Mitchell reached behind him for the two small plastic paddles they found in the chaos of the first hour aboard the raft. He passed them over to Dale, sitting near the flap.

Rowing would be difficult, but it gave the crew some much needed hope and something to do. Dale and Cally laid down on their stomachs with their head and shoulders out of the raft and paddled as best as they could. Sometimes they also sat at the edge of the raft to row. With adrenalin pumping, the exuberant crew rowed hard toward land. The sun felt good on their cold, tired bodies.

Panic was beginning to set in after trying the cell phones one more time. Mindy tried to calm herself with words of self-encouragement.

*You're doing fine Mindy. Everything's fine. Just run down to the docks. They'll be right in. Any time now.*

Multiple scenarios floated through her mind as to why Dale hadn't called. These ideas were now fluctuating wildly with harsh rebukes toward her husband. She mumbled to herself about what she wanted to say to Dale.

*You better not have screwed up, Dale Pruitt. Get my damn kids home to me now please. We'll worry about the ass kickin' I'm going to give you later. Just get 'em home please.*

Having already left her truck down at the cannery for Dale and the kids to get home in, she jumped into the second car and pulled nervously down Pruitt Lane toward Lake View Drive. She took a right onto the dirt road toward Otmeloi Road that would take her to Spruce Cape and onto Woodland Drive which was one of her waiting spots. Over the years Mindy had found two or three favorite spots to sit and wait for Dale to come home. In the early days she did so as a lonely fisherman's wife waiting for her man to return. In recent years, however the moments had been family affairs. Mindy would load Mitch and Calista in the car and wait for Dad to come home. She was daydreaming of such special times when she pulled up to her Spruce Cape waiting spot and stared out at a vast, and empty, Gulf of Alaska.

Turning the car off, she tried Calista's cell phone one more time. Same result.

*Where the hell is my family? Dale you better call me!*

Mindy stayed for what seemed to her to be an hour, but was probably closer to fifteen minutes. She started the car and pulled back onto the road that skirted Spruce Cape. She turned back toward town. She'd go to the cannery and then to her spot on Near Island. She'd find them.

*That "sat" phone is down and he can't get hold of me. That's all. He's probably shaking in his boots scared of what's going to happen when he finally does get hold of me.*

Mindy was verging on panic. Something was wrong; that she was sure of. But it wasn't anything that Dale couldn't handle. Dale had his faults and she was often frustrated by him over the years, but he would let nothing happen to his kids; she was certain of this.

Somehow, Mindy found herself pulling into her parking spot at work. She hadn't planned on coming into work on this day, but "auto-pilot" had steered her there. Now that she was here she decided to go in.

"Hey! What are you doing here?" The voice came from the behind the computer screen.

"Dad, we're not getting anywhere."

Dale saw that Mitchell was right. About an hour before, Cali had said they were getting closer. They had argued over the last few hours. Were they getting closer? Farther away? They didn't know for sure. But Dale could see that they weren't really making much progress. They had been fighting wind and current almost all of the time. The effort and the lack of food and water had beaten them down as well. Dale was still experiencing hypothermic symptoms. He shivered uncontrollably at times, suffered drowsiness, had pale and cold skin, and had twice been jolted from a state of unconsciousness. But the paddling had been good. He felt better now. But still he knew Mitchell was right.

He was lying back in the raft. Mitchell and Cally were at the opening to the tent, slapping away at the ocean surface two feet below. Riding a couple of feet above the surface made it difficult for the paddlers to get any leverage from their strokes. They made the best of it though. No one slacked during their shift. When it was their turn each crew member gave it everything they had. After all, it was land that they could see. Home. Kodiak.

The Red River is located on the southwest coast of Kodiak Island, between Bumble Bay and Low Cape. It is on the opposite side of the island from the town of Kodiak which is in the northeast. The land that they could see was as far away from their home as one could possibly get on the island. But that didn't stop them. They had seen land. They would do anything in their power to get there.

Dale knew that Mitchell was right. He figured that each rowing shift had been about fifteen minutes and they had switched over twenty times. By these calculations, Dale estimated that they had rowed for about five hours.

The land appeared to be about the same distance away as it had at the beginning. Dale kept this to himself as the crew paddled on.

Mindy stayed at work only long enough to shuffle some papers around her desk and tell Nick that the family had not returned. Then she left.

She drove through downtown Kodiak, made a quick left and then a right onto Shelikof Street. To her left was the small boat harbor. The harbor which is owned and operated by the City of Kodiak has been functioning as a top-producing commercial fishing port since the early twentieth century. Mindy looked at the *Calista Marie* moored in her berth at the harbor and wished that Dale and the kids had not taken the *Magnum*.

She continued along Shelikof Street. Skirting the harbor, she approached the section that housed most of Kodiak's canneries. The Ocean Beauty is located with the harbor on one side and Shelikof Street on the other. A few parking places were available out front. Mindy's truck still sat in one of the spaces.

She pulled her car around and nosed up to the building to see an empty dock. No *Magnum*. No boat of any kind.

*What in the hell is going on?*

Quickly she backed up and turned around in the direction she had come. On the Zharoff Bridge she craned her neck to get a glimpse of the channel far below. Nothing.

Once across the bridge and onto Near Island, Mindy eased her car around to her other favorite waiting spot. She left the car, walked to the lookout spot and sat down on a large rock. Looking out over the channel that leads from Chiniak Bay to Marmot Bay and ultimately to the Gulf of Alaska, Mindy saw nothing. No boats coming, none going.

She called Tim Blott again.

"Hi Tim. It's Mindy Pruitt."

Hi Mindy."

"Have you heard from Dale yet?"

"No Mindy, not yet. Nothing on your end either huh?"

"No, nothing here. I'm sitting on Near Island and they're not coming down the channel yet. I don't know what's going on."

No reply. Only silence.

"Tim I need you to start calling around. Call the fleet and find someone who knows where the hell Dale is."

"I've already made a couple calls Mindy, but...."

"Have you called Mitch Kepplinger or Phil?"

"No, I haven't called them yet. I can do that for you. What about the Coast Guard Mindy?"

"Yeah, I've been thinking about that too Tim. I've been thinking it's probably about time. Something's wrong."

Paddling at the life raft flap, Cally turned to look inside.

"Uncle Dale I can't see the land anymore"

"Yeah, it's gone Dad.  Those clouds lowered down over there and it's gone."

"We can just keep paddling that way."  Calista said, pointing straight through the opening in the flap.

"We don't know which way 'that way' is Calista," Dale said.  "After a while we could get turned around and be paddling in the wrong direction."

"I know Dad, but we can't quit.  We can't give up!"

"We're not giving up Calista.  We're just not doing this anymore.  It's a waste of our strength."

Then he said the thing he'd been thinking for several hours and had held back to keep the positive vibe alive as long as possible.

"We can't paddle all the way over there.  It's too far and the current and wind in this place will not let us do that.  Not happening."

Dale was surprised at the reaction of his crew.  Not a word.  There was no arguing or complaining.  Just silence.  They had known for hours too.  Nobody had wanted to be the one to say it.

The paddling had given them hope and lifted their spirits, but they gave up. Mitchell went to close the flap as Calista lay back with Dale. As he reached his head out one last time he felt a drop from above.

"Dad, it's raining!"

# CHAPTER TWELVE

"United States Coast Guard Kodiak Division, how can I help you?"

"Uh..........hi my husband and my kids are missing." Her voice was hesitant.

"Ma'am you're going to need to be a little more specific. Where were they?"

"They're the crew of the *F/V Magnum*. They've been fishing along the mainland, somewhere near Jute Bay. He called and told me they were coming home on Wednesday night."

"And where did they say they were coming to?"

"Kodiak. The Ocean Beauty is our cannery. My husband's name is Dale Pruitt. He's been fishing these waters for over twenty years. I'm sure it's just a misunderstanding or something, but I'm getting really worried here and I don't know where they are."

"Is Dale often late like this?"

"Well I guess like all fishermen around here, sometimes you find more fish or need to duck out of the weather or something. He's like all the rest I guess. The boat he's on, *The Magnum*, it's a leased boat. It's his first trip out on this boat. Can you find them for me please?"

"Well first off Mrs. Pruitt we're going to need to find out if these people are really missing and not just holed up somewhere."

"Listen Mr. Whatever your name was, let me tell you something. 'These people' are my family and I need you to find them."

Robinette worried as she approached her house. A busy day at work had kept her mind off the fact that Mindy had not called. The last thing she said to her as she left yesterday had been *call me when the kiddos get home.*

Robinette had been too busy at work to take a lunch that morning. *Good day to be busy* she thought as she walked through her unlocked front door. The phone was ringing.

"Dang," she said softly to herself. She had just stopped at home to grab another coat and head back to work. She looked at the ringing phone and thought about not picking it up.

*I have a lot of work to do back there. Let it ring.*

She was ready to walk out the door when suddenly she stepped back to the phone and picked it up.

"Hello.".

"Robinette? Hi this is Janetta."

Immediately Robinette knew something was wrong; she could hear the strain in her friend's voice.

"Have you talked to Mindy?" Robinette's heart sank. "They're looking for Dale. He's got all the kids with him, Robinette."

"Oh my God," Robinette nearly dropped the phone. She tried to remember what time Mindy had told her they were supposed to be home.

*Weren't they supposed to be back yesterday? They've been lost for over 24 hours.*

Janetta was talking on the other end of the line.

"The whole fleet is calling around and asking who's seen Dale and no one's seen him Robinette. He's got all the kids. Have you talked to Mindy?" She repeated the question.

"Janetta I need to go. I don't know anything. This is the first I've heard. I need to call her right now. Thanks"

Robinette hung up the phone. She picked it back up immediately and dialed the house.

*Hi you've reached the Pruitt home......* Click.

She dialed Mindy's cell phone.

"Hello." Her voice sounded distant, but focused.

"Hey Mindy, it's Robinette. Where are you?"

"Oh I'm driving down to the waterfront again."

"I talked to Janetta Min. You OK?"

"I've been better Robinette."

"Who's with you?"

"Nobody."

"You know Min; I'm not so sure you should be alone. Why don't you go home. I'll meet you there."

"Yeah OK, I think that's a good idea. I'll meet you at the house."

"OK sweetie. You be careful. Just go home and I'll meet you there. We'll take it from there OK?"

"OK." Matter of factly, Mindy pulled the car over, waited for one car to pass and then did a U-turn on Mill Bay Road.

Robinette grabbed her coat and hot-footed it to her car.

The rain that was falling in the Shelikof Strait was nothing more than a light drizzle. But the good news was that water began accumulating in the catch as it was designed to do.

"Dad, we saw this movie in class and they were talking about how you shouldn't drink the first couple of loads. The rain needs to rinse the salt spray off."

"Have guys died from doing that?" Calista responded.

"Well, probably, since you can dehydrate much faster from drinking salt water much faster. We gotta make sure the water is fresh when we drink it."

"I'm so thirsty Dad"

"Calista, Mitch is right. Dump the first one for sure. We'll see after that.

Calista did as she was told. She opened the spigot, filled a cup from the emergency kit, reached out through the small opening in the flap and dumped the water.

"I can't believe I just dumped water into the ocean when we're so thirsty."

"It's still raining Calista. It's going to clean it off for us and leave a little to drink. It's not raining much though so get moving."

Quickly she filled another cup and repeated this process several times. From the sound of the rain on the canopy the crew could tell the rain was subsiding. They needed to make the best of it now.

"Let me taste this one." Calista handed the cup to Dale. It was an eight ounce cup. Half full. He took a sip. "I think it's OK" He took another small drink and handed the cup to Calista.

"There are two other people so just take your share." Mitchell and Cally watched intently as Calista took her sip.

She handed the cup to Cally who took a sip and handed it to Mitchell who finished it off.

The water was like a gift from God. They had been fighting for their lives for about 45 hours cramped together in this tiny floating tent. Needless to say, the water tasted heavenly. It also boosted their mood and restored hope.

The energy boost didn't last long when they realized that the rain had stopped. One cup of fresh water would be it for the time being.

"The rain'll come back soon guys and we'll be ready when it does. We know how to do it now."

"Are they going to come for us Uncle Dale? They gotta know we're out here don't they?"

"Yeah, they'll be on their way out here soon. We gotta be around 35 hours overdue. They'll be out soon. I just hope they look in the right place. We're a long way from Jute Bay."

# CHAPTER THIRTEEN

"They didn't come home." Mindy's voice was emotionless and factual. She got out of her car and walked toward Robinette who was already at the house and waiting on the front step as Mindy had driven up.

"They didn't come home." She repeated.

Robinette said nothing. She enveloped Mindy in a deep, heartfelt hug.

"Where the hell are they Rob?" Mindy looked deep into her friend's eyes as the two turned and walked into the house. "Let's go back down to the waterfront and look for them."

"A lot of people are looking for them Mindy. I think we should just chill out here for a while. Let's just sit down and figure out what to do."

She led Mindy into the kitchen. The centerpiece of the room is a large island. The kitchen is Pruitt central when family is present. Dale and Mindy both love to cook. Most meals are eaten bellied up to the island in the middle of the kitchen.

Mindy settled onto a stool as Robinette dropped a couple of ice cubes in a glass and filled it with water from the tap. She set the glass down in front of her.

Robinette had been trying to get up the nerve to tell Mindy that they needed to call the Coast Guard. Kodiak is a blue collar town. The Pruitts are a hard-nosed family. To call the Coast Guard for help is not something to be considered except as a last resort. Mindy's entire family was a full day past due. Robinette knew there was a problem. She felt strongly that now was the time to bring in the professionals.

"We need to call the Coast Guard." Mindy surprised her with her answer.

"Well I've already done it Robinette and I have a big problem with the little jerk that answered the phone."

"Why? What happened?"

"Well when I told them the situation he told me that 'we need to find out if these people are really missing'. I think I hung up on him."

"So are they looking for them?"

"I don't know. That little guy pissed me off Robinette. This is my family we're talking about here."

"I know hun. We're going to need to call them back and see what they're doing."

Back at the sink now refilling Mindy's water Robinette looked out the kitchen window to see Susie Pruitt walking toward them on Pruitt Lane from her place down the road. James Pruitt's mom, Susie is the ex-wife of Dale's brother Sid. She walked in without knocking.

"Oh Mindy!" she cried as she gave her a long embrace. "Yorg called and said it's all over the radios out there. Have you heard anything?"

"No, nothing yet Susie. Thanks for coming over."

"Mindy! My goodness!" She was incredulous. "Have you called the Coast Guard yet? We need to call the Coast Guard."

"We were just talking about that Susie," Robinette jumped in. "Mindy already called them……"

"Yeah, and I'm pissed at them too."

"You're pissed at *him* Mindy. It wasn't them, it was just him."

"What happened?" Susie inquired.

"The guy told me that he had to find out if *these people are really missing.*" Each time she said it the level of anger increased in her voice.

"Well we need to call back right now. They need to get out there and find them. It's been too long."

Susie picked up the phone.

"Mindy, what's the number?"

Susie followed Mindy's instructions and dialed up Coast Guard Air Station Kodiak. With the phone ringing, Susie passed the receiver to Robinette. With a puzzled look she took the phone and held it to her ear.

"Hello. Is this the Coast Guard?" She glanced from Susie and then to Mindy. "My name is Robinette and I'm a friend of Mindy Pruitt. She called about an hour ago to report her family missing."

Mindy and Susie watched anxiously as Robinette listened to the Coast Guard Ensign on the other end of the line.

"OK, well again my name is Robinette and we'll be waiting for that call. Thank you so much."

She hung up the phone and went to the sink for more water. Susie and Mindy waited tensely for her to deliver the news. She took a quick sip of water and then turned to them.

"They're getting ready to launch the search and rescue. They're going to call us as soon as they've begun."

"Oh my God." Mindy slumped her head down onto the cold tile of the kitchen island. Susie and Robinette moved to either side of her and held her close.

Mindy had been in denial up till now. She had gone through multiple possibilities in her mind explaining away the fact that they were late. Dale had been late plenty of times before. It's a very unpredictable way of making a living; a very unpredictable lifestyle.

Leaning against the kitchen island, flanked by life-long friends, Mindy began to break her denial defenses. She finally conceded that her family was in a very serious situation. When the Coast Guard gets involved in Kodiak, people know it's for real.

While her friends comforted her with words of encouragement, she felt like she had two choices at this point: She could break down or she could step up and fight on. She chose the latter.

"Can you guys cancel whatever you have going and stay with me right now? I don't want to be alone."

"Of course honey."

"Already done."

"I love you guys. We're going to be OK. They're going to be OK."

"Of course they are Mindy."

"Robinette, call Tanya and Rhoda please. I want them here too."

"OK Mindy, I'll do that. And how about some provisions? We're going to need a few things so I'll run to the store and make those calls."

"Mindy and I will stay here and settle in to wait for that call from the Coast Guard," said Susie.

"Perfect. You take care now Mindy and I'll be right back. We're going to beat this thing." Robinette then pulled away from the house and left Mindy and Susie behind.

Several hours of silence passed in the raft. This day had been better than the last. They had seen land and drank water. The amount of water collected was far from what was needed, but it was heartening nonetheless. Any left over excitement from the day had evaporated. The crew had grown quiet.

Calista was snuggling with Dale. She quietly asked him questions from time to time. Finally Cally broke the silence.

"When we get home, I am so going to eat chicken strips at Henrys. That's going to be good." No reply. "What are you guys going to do first?"

"I'm going to tell your Aunt and your mom and dad that I'm sorry," Dale said sorrowfully.

"I don't think you'll be needin' to do that Uncle Dale. It's going to be such a celebration. They're going to be so happy. They won't be expecting an apology."

"Yeah but Cally, the celebration's going to end sometime and Miss Mindy's still gonna be mad at me; best to tell her *sorry*."

"I'm going to give Candice a hug."

"Great Mitch, you're going to give her a hug before Mom."

"I didn't say that Calista. Geez, go back to sleep."

"I wasn't sleeping, for your information, Mitch. I've been sitting over here making sure Dad is OK the whole time. All you've been doing is sitting over there saying nothing."

"Leave me alone please."

"Well I am going to drink a gallon of apple juice. I am so craving apple juice."

"Yeah I think you already told us that, thanks."

"Mitchell, that's enough. Will you two stop it please? That's not helping." Dale didn't move a muscle during this admonishment.

*PAN PAN............PAN PAN........PAN PAN........This is Coast Guard Air Station Kodiak calling all stations. Please be advised that the 57 foot F/V Magnum and her four man crew are overdue into Kodiak. Position of the vessel is currently unknown. Last known position of the Magnum is*

*approximately one mile off Jute Bay. Anyone with knowledge pertaining to the F/V Magnum and her crew should call Coast Guard Air Station Kodiak.*

*PAN PAN...........PAN PAN.........PAN PAN.........This is Coast Guard Air Station Kodiak calling all stations. Please be advised that the 57 foot F/V Magnum and her four man crew are overdue into Kodiak. Position of the vessel is currently unknown. Last known position of the Magnum is approximately one mile off Jute Bay. Anyone with knowledge pertaining to the F/V Magnum and her crew should call Coast Guard Air Station Kodiak.*

*PAN PAN...........PAN PAN.........PAN PAN.........This is Coast Guard Air Station Kodiak calling all stations. Please be advised that the 57 foot F/V Magnum and her four man crew are overdue into Kodiak. Position of the vessel is currently unknown. Last known position of the Magnum is approximately one mile off Jute Bay. Anyone with knowledge pertaining to the F/V Magnum and her crew should call Coast Guard Air Station Kodiak.*

Fisherman and family friend, Steve Russell was on his boat fishing near Kodiak when he heard the Coast Guard distress message coming over the radio. PAN PAN is the signal that the Coast Guard uses to alert the fleet to an emergency. A MAY DAY is used when there are known potential victims of an urgent disaster.

Since the Magnum was only missing, a PAN PAN was used to alert any boats in the area to the situation. Steve knew that Dale had leased the Magnum. He knew who Dale had on the boat with him.

"Oh my goodness." He muttered to himself as he turned to his nephew who was fishing with him. "Come on Kevin. We're going in."

Steve and his nephew quickly secured the nets on deck and headed toward the harbor.

# CHAPTER FOURTEEN

Robinette stood trying to make her mind up in the wine aisle of the Safeway.

*Is it appropriate for the situation? This is pretty serious and we need clear heads. On the other hand, we'll be celebrating soon so it would be good to have on hand.*

She grabbed a couple of bottles and put them in her cart. As she put snack foods like sodas, chips, and veggie trays in the basket it was as if she were shopping for a party. She fervently hoped this would be true. She planned to hit the Pizza Hut on the way back to the house.

Word of a boat overdue always spreads quickly in Kodiak. At any given time, a good percentage of Kodiak fishermen are out working the seas while monitoring activity on their VHF radios. They then phone their wives or girlfriends. In a matter of minutes, word is out in the streets of the close community.

This town rallies for their distressed brethren during such times. The wives at home are comforted by friends and family, while the Coast Guard and local fishermen work to find the missing. Sometimes they're found quickly, sometimes not at all.

Robinette knew that this was going to be huge on the island as she made her way through the check stand. She made polite small talk with the checker, but didn't mention Dale. She was curious to see if the checker had heard yet. Apparently she hadn't. Robinette said a quick prayer of thanks for that. She had seen Kodiak lose crews of fishermen plenty of times. Joyous times of rescue were interspersed as well. But this was different. This was a family. Most in town will understand she thought, but Dale's going to be in question for taking the kids out with him. Rumors will fly. Some will support him; some will give him hell. Everyone will want to have them safely home. That was the bottom line.

Robinette rushed out of the Safeway, hopped in her car and headed for pizza. She was hurrying as fast as she could.

Pulling up to the house she noticed Felicia's car outside. When she walked in she noticed that Felicia was covered in grass clippings.

"Looking good hun." She said trying to keep the mood light.

"Thanks Robinette, I was mowing when Daniel called. I came right over. Mindy's in the dining room."

Mindy was sitting at the dining room table with Susie. Her cell phone rang. She answered before the first ring had finished.

"Hello!" It was Tim Blott from the cannery looking for information. "Nothing yet Tim. I'll keep you posted and you do the same OK?"

Susie's phone rang. It was James. James had been at the house when his friend had called with the news. He didn't believe it so he called his mom. She had confirmed his fear.

Felicia's cell phone rang, and then Robinette's. It was going to be a long night. Felicia announced that she had to run home to shower. She said she'd be right back.

"Felicia, say a prayer before you go." The voice was soft, not obviously directed toward anyone. It seemed to be more of a spoken thought. Mindy hadn't moved her head or looked in anyone's direction when she said it. The four women in the room bowed their heads as Felicia began to pray. Afterwards, Felicia left the house in a subdued silence.

"We've got to get a handle on this situation." Robinette stepped in. "No call from the Coast Guard yet?"

"No."

"Give me that house phone. I'm calling them right now." She dialed the Coast Guard.

"Hi this is Robinette Sagalkin. I'm representing the Pruitt family. Do you have any information for me? Are you looking for the crew?"

The voice at the other end of the phone said that a Commander Trippert wanted to talk to her.

"Hello Mrs. Sagalkin. This is Lieutenant Commander Trippert, United States Coast Guard Sector Juneau. I'm here to help you and the Pruitt family through this."

"Well thank you Commander. Please call me Robinette."

"OK, that'll be good Robin and you can call me Todd. I know the family has made a few calls to us. How have you felt about our service so far?"

"Well Mindy was a little peeved with something one of the guys said, but we're not worrying about that now. We just want them back."

"That's what we want too, Robin. From here on out I will be the person that you can direct all communications to. I'm going to give you my extension here at the office, as well as, my personal cell phone number. You or Mrs. Pruitt can call me at anytime for any reason."

"Thank you so much Comman....... uh I mean Todd."

"You're welcome. In the past ten minutes, out of Kodiak we've deployed one Jayhawk helicopter and one Dolphin helicopter to the area. Within the next 20 minutes the Cutter *Spar* will depart to conduct a search of the coastline on the mainland. We'll also have an HC130 fixed-wing aircraft in the air momentarily. The search is in full gear and we're going to do everything within our power to bring this family home."

"You're a Godsend Todd."

"It's what we're here for Robin. I need to get back to work here, but feel free to call anytime like I said."

Robinette missed most of the final comments by Commander Trippert because Mindy was talking to her.

"Rob, tell him we only want to talk to them."

In the few minutes since Felicia had left and Robinette was on the phone with the Coast Guard, cell phones in the room had rung four more times. Mindy knew that rumors would be flying soon. She only wanted to get her information from the Coast Guard. She continued talking to Robinette while she was on the phone.

"We only want to talk to the Coast Guard," Mindy repeated.

Holding the phone between her shoulder and ear Robinette looked over to Mindy as she was speaking to her.

"Uh, Todd. Before you go, Mindy has requested that we only talk to you about the search and rescue.

She's worried about rumors and such that will be flying around Kodiak soon. We're just going to get all of our information from you if that's OK."

"That's perfect Robin. It's just the way we like it. Now you take care of Mindy and we'll do what we can to take care of her family."

"That's wonderful. Thank you Todd. We'll talk soon."

"OK. Bye now."

Robinette noticed that Susie and Mindy were looking at her.

"Search is in progress hun. They have helicopters, a plane and a cutter on the way."

"They're probably sitting on the beach telling stories and waiting for them. Might have found them already."

Mindy said, "I need to call Mom and Dad."

Gordon Graham nearly passed out at the news from his daughter, Mindy. With a shaky hand, he scribbled the names on a slip of paper; Dale, Cally Rose, Mitchell, and Calista. *Oh my gosh.........* He managed to write the raw details of what he was hearing. Boat missing, Coast Guard searching. With difficulty, he managed to hang up the phone and contact his wife Patsy at a friend's house. He simply told her to come home now. Sensing the urgency, Patsy rushed home.

Gordon sat slumped at the dining room table when his wife returned home.

"What's going on Gordon?" He gestured to the sheet of paper sitting next to the phone and Patsy read the news. She immediately called her son, John. Within the hour, he was at the house and ready to run her to SEA/TAC airport.

In a state of mounting anxiety, Patsy waited on standby for a flight to Anchorage. John agreed to look after his father, Gordon, while she was away. This fact helped marginally calm her as she waited. Gordon was in no shape to travel after hearing this news. Knowing that their son would be with him comforted her. Her energy was now turned toward her daughter, Mindy Pruitt. Her family was missing and Patsy wanted to be with her. She was anxious to depart. She needed to be there for Mindy. Whatever the news, she needed to be with her.

She waited through a long night before finally catching a Saturday morning flight to Kodiak.

# CHAPTER FIFTEEN

Mitchell thought he heard something.

Craning his head out from under the tent flap he noticed that the fog had become dense. Visibility was perhaps two hundred feet.

"Dad, I think I heard something. I think it was a plane, or a boat or something."

"What is it Mit...?"

"Shhhh!" Mitchell turned and held his finger to his lips.

The crew sat extra quiet as Mitchell opened the flap more for better hearing. They exchanged hopeful glances around the cramped quarters on the tiny raft.

"Definitely Dad." Mitchell was sure he heard a motor. It was faint, and he didn't know if it was boat or plane, but he heard something.

"It's a plane," Calista chimed in, "I can hear a plane."

A cautious cheer broke out in the raft.

"I think she's right Uncle Dale. Should we shoot a flare?"

"I don't know Cally. We only have two more. We shouldn't waste them. I do hear something though. They're looking for us now."

"I think that's more than one plane. Mitchell, look out and see if you can see something."

"I'm already here Dad. I don't see anything. The clouds are really heavy. They're close, I can hear them."

"Let's shoot a flare Dad."

"Yeah, Uncle Dale. She's right. Let's shoot one." Cally reached behind her head and grabbed the flare gun. She handed it to Dale who had scooted himself upright and over toward the tent flap.

Mitchell moved away from the opening replacing Dale on the other side of the raft.

Dale knew that it'd be a one in a million shot to put this flare up in the sight line of a plane crossing the Strait in this pea soup fog. He figured that the Coast Guard would probably begin their search up near Jute Bay, their last known location. That was miles from where they were now.

But, caught up in the moment and eager to keep the light of hope alive, Dale reached out and fired the flare upward in the direction of the sound of the plane.

The crew waited in silence. Nothing.

Back at her home, Felicia spent what seemed to be 15 minutes with the warm shower running over her head and shoulders, praying.

She turned off the water, stepped out, grabbed a towel and felt like a new person. She had needed to talk to God and the shower had provided the perfect environment. Deeply spiritual and strong in faith, Felicia felt rejuvenated.

"They're going to be OK." She said to herself in the mirror as she dried and got dressed.

Felicia could hear the voices in the other room as she opened the door. In the living room of her Mill Bay home was her son Paul and several of his friends. They were all talking anxiously about the overdue crew.

"Mom what's going on with the Pruitts?"

"Well hun, Dale and the kids are overdue

"How late are they?"

"I guess about thirty hours or so."

"Wow. Mom, Monica (Felicia's youngest daughter) wants to have Candice over. You mind if a few people come to hang out at the house?"

"No, that's fine. Mindy needs me over there so whatever you need to do, honey. Remember you have to get ready for your run tomorrow."

"Yeah Mom I need to go to Kodiak Marine for some supplies."

"OK Honey, we'll go in the morning. Then I'll drop you off at the dock. What time are they expecting you?"

"I think 9 or 10. I'll let you know."

"Keep it positive over here OK? Dale and the kids are going to be just fine." Felecia gave her son a hug and left the house. She experienced a surge of hope as she started the car.

"They're going to be OK." She kept repeating as she backed out of the driveway. Every bone in her body yearned for this to be true.

When Felicia walked in the Pruitt home there were seven or eight people in the living room and two more in the kitchen. Most of them were talking on their cell phones. Two phones rang simultaneously in the living room before she was able to reach Robinette in the dining room. She was on the phone with Commander Trippert.

"OK Todd, well thanks for the update. I'm sure I'll be calling back soon."

Holding the phone between her ear and shoulder she glanced over at Felicia and held a finger in the air to signal, 'wait a minute'.

"Yes sir. She has requested that I be the spokesperson. We're flooded with calls here, but we're going to try to keep this line open." She paused. "Todd, you are our information source. Unless it comes from you, we're treating it as if it weren't true."

Feeling like the phone conversation wasn't finished, Felicia went to the kitchen and grabbed a glass of water. She said hello to a couple leaning against the counter. Mindy was nowhere to be seen. The doorbell rang.

"Todd, thank you so much. We really appreciate what you're doing. I should be the one who answers when you call. If someone else answers I'd appreciate it if you asked for me. This place is filling up." She looked over to see four more people coming into the living room. "Thanks again Todd. Talk to you soon."

Hanging up the phone she swung around the corner into the kitchen grabbing Felicia by the arm.

"Come on." She pushed her toward the stairs without saying a word to the growing contingent of supporters. "She's upstairs with Tanya, Rhoda, and Susie."

The two women paused outside the closed door to Dale and Mindy's master bedroom. Robinette tapped quietly on the door and went in without waiting for an answer. Mindy was lying back on the bed with her feet on the floor staring blankly up at the ceiling.

"I need to go back down there." She said to no one in particular.

"You don't *need* to do anything Mindy. Those people are there for you. You don't need to entertain them for Christ's sake."

While Felicia was home taking a shower, Mindy had become overwhelmed with so many people in the house. She said she needed some time alone and headed upstairs to her room. They had been making small talk when Felicia and Robinette came in.

Mindy raised herself to a sitting position on the edge of the bed. She looked at her friends and said, "Let's pray."

The women gathered in a circle holding hands.

"Mindy you get in the middle. We'll pray around you."

Mindy did as she was told. The friends closed the circle around her with held hands. The prayer circle was focused. These women of faith were ready to bring God into the equation. They all believed that He was running the show, but each felt they could do more to get closer to Him. Felicia began to pray out loud.

*Dear Glorious God, moments like these have a way of reminding us that everything we have and everything we are.............*

With tightly held hands and closed eyes, the support group said *Amen* in unison. The prayer gave them all strength. Mindy in particular felt rejuvenated. She opened the door and led the group down the stairs to meet the growing crowd of supporters, well-wishers and friends.

# CHAPTER SIXTEEN

"OK, so that was probably a stupid move."

After what seemed to be three or four minutes, Dale finally broke the silence. They were still hearing the faint hum of engines around them, but it was pretty obvious at this point that no one had seen their flare. The Captain wasn't surprised, given the weather conditions.

"You pretty much have to have a plane in sight to get lucky enough to have someone see a flare in this shit."

Dale gave the crew a pep talk insofar as he was able. "It's OK guys. They're looking for us now. We'll be found soon."

He closed the flap and worked his way back into position. Four bodies lying side by side. So close, yet so far away.

A heavy silence hung over the cramped quarters of the Pruitt's life raft. Hope and optimism was in short supply though. They were pretty sure the search for them was on, but the long hauls in the small boat were taking their toll. Each crew member pondered their mortality and the possibility that they weren't going to make it home.

In the silence, they heard another engine. A plane? Mitchell quickly pushed himself over to the flap and peered outside. He could see nothing except a marine layer and waves lapping up against the craft. He stayed there for five minutes or so looking out at the nothingness. Hoping.

"I think my mind's starting to play tricks on me" he said without emotion as he took his spot back in the row of bodies. "This sucks."

The Little Bar at the Elks Club was half-full with the usual collection of Friday night regulars. Upstairs, the Friday night senior's club was having dinner as usual. This night, of course, was different than most. By this time, there was hardly a soul in Kodiak who wasn't aware of the frantic search for the Pruitts. All conversations were about the missing crew. Some speculated about their location.   Others predicted morbid outcomes. Some told stories of friends and loved ones who were lost at sea.   Nearly everyone in Kodiak had lost a friend or family member to the sea.

All conversation stopped, however, when a gentleman at the bar ended a cell phone conversation, stood up on his bar stool and announced to the patrons that the Coast Guard had, 'found four bodies'.

After some initial shock and tears, many of the patrons got on their cell phones to spread the news. One gentleman ran upstairs to tell the seniors there. So distraught they were at the news, they left in the middle of dinner.

In minutes, word that the Pruitts were dead had spread through town.   The Pruitt home was Grand Central Station for the information onslaught.

Gradually, people in the house began to whisper the news back and forth.   Most worried about Mindy and tried to keep the news under wraps.   Unfortunately, others weren't so discreet and Mindy overheard.

"They found four bodies."

"No I heard it was three bodies and a survival suit."

"No way man, I heard it from my Uncle and he's out with the fleet.   It was four bodies."

Felicia's cell phone rang and she saw on the display that it was her husband Daniel. He had been monitoring the radios from his fishing boat. She pulled Rhoda out on the deck with her by the arm.

"Hi Dan, what's up?  People are saying they found bodies, is that true?"

"Haven't heard that, but I think they found his seine in the water."

"What does that mean Dan?"  She shouted into the phone. The strain was getting to her. She was in serious danger of losing it.

"It could mean that they went down, Felicia. It could also mean he dumped it.  Not sure right now."

"I'll call you later Dan."

Felicia hung up and told Rhoda what Dan had told her.  In a brief, despairing moment, the two friends embraced; sobbing out on the deck where Mindy couldn't see them. They then remembered their reason for being there.

"We're here for Mindy.  We need to pull ourselves together.  This doesn't mean anything.  We don't even know if it's true.  We need to call the Coast Guard." They repeated to each other, nodding like bobble head dolls to reassure themselves.

They went back into the house full of people. They found their way through the crowd to see that Robinette was already on the phone with Commander Trippert.

"Uh huh." She looked over at them with raised eyebrows. "So, no bodies, but you saw debris?" The crowd hushed as she spoke on the phone trying to hear what was being said. "Well Todd, I have to tell you that rumors are out of control around here. We're only listening to you. We'll keep checking for that email and get back to you when we get it. Thank you Todd."

As she hung up the phone she wiped an escaping tear from her eyes and squared her shoulders back to speak to the waiting crowd.

"OK guys! There are no bodies. You know why there are no bodies? There are no bodies because they're OK and they're going to stay that way. We need to get off the phones because people do not know what the hell's going on around here. Only the Coast Guard knows."

Just then Mindy entered the room from the kitchen. Her friends had been amazed at her strength. She had been totally put together. But her face was worried. She looked dog-tired. Tension was written on her brow.

"What's going on? Tell me the truth Robinette. What did he say?"

Across town, Shawn and Jeff Holden embraced and cried together.

"We should go over to the house and be with Mindy," Shawn said.

"The last thing she needs is us blubbering around her, honey. I called and told Robinette to tell her we're there for her. She said she'd give her the message. It sounded like there were a lot of people there. We don't need to go."

The couple had agonized since hearing the news that Dale and the kids were missing. Their suffering was as if it were their own children lost out there. They also worried whether they should even tell their son, Michael.

Mitchell's best friend, Michael Holden, was now in the Coast Guard.

"We should tell him. He deserves to know."

"Jeff, Michael might be out there looking for them right now. If he knows it's Mitch and Calista I don't know if he could do it."

"I suppose you're right honey. Maybe we should just wait."

Jeff continued to hug his wife. Through the window, he could see his pickup truck sitting outside their home. Months prior, Calista had painted him a message on the back window of his camper shell. The message said *I Love Farva – CMP*. In place of the word love, she had drawn a big heart.

The kids called Jeff, Farva. The nickname came from the movie, *Super Troopers*. Seeing the message that Calista had written was too much for Jeff to take. He closed the blinds and cried.

"The rumor about bodies is not true. It's not true Mindy," she repeated. "The C-130 did spot some debris which they think might be Dale's seine. A helicopter is on the scene. They're taking a picture of the net to email to us. They want us to see if we can identify it."

Mindy stared numbly showing no reaction to what she was hearing. Silently she walked through the crowd of people, opened the sliding glass door leading to the deck, walked to the rail and bent over to let out a bellow of despair that she had been locked deep inside. Robinette and Felicia quickly followed her, closing the sliding door behind them. The other supporters gave them their space and stayed inside.

Mindy was leaning her head and shoulders out over the railing and bawling to the universe.

"No GOD! Not my children! Please, please, no, no. Not my children God."

Robinette and Felicia stood with their wounded friend. After a couple of minutes they began soothing her as best they could.

"Get it out Mindy. You need to get it out."

"Actually Mindy, I think you need to stop. You need to knock it off. We need to stay positive and this isn't helping. You need to keep it together."

"It's OK Mindy," Felicia countered as the sobbing continued.

"Mindy, that's enough!" scolded Robinette, "this is good news. The rumors were just that. They didn't find any bodies. You know why? Because there aren't any, that's why. They're fine! The Coast Guard is going to find them so just knock it off."

Robinette's mild scolding had its effect. Immediately, Mindy stopped crying, wiped her eyes, and stood-up tall.

"I want these cell phones gone." She demanded.

With that she walked, now composed, back into the house. Felicia followed her and then Robinette followed her. Robinette raised her voice to get the attention of the crowd.

"Alright everybody, new rule! Cell phones need to disappear. We don't want ring tones and we don't want people talking on their phones. If you need to talk on the phone please go outside. These rumors are getting out of control. The only phone that's going to be in use is the house phone. The only person we're talking to is the Coast Guard Commander. There have been no bodies found because there aren't any bodies, dammit! We're keeping it positive in here people. Mindy needs us to be strong."

Robinette had officially taken charge of the operation and Felicia was relieved about this. The crowd of people at the house was a mixed bag. Most were friends there to show support, but it seemed to be entertainment for some hangers on. Robinette put Mindy's nephew in charge of crowd control at the front door.

"Make sure everyone who comes in knows that cell phones are turned off."

Meanwhile, Susie was talking to her son, James.

"The Coast Guard is emailing a picture of the seine that they found for us to identify. Do you know what it looks like?"

"Heck yeah Mom, I spent all last week on the boat getting it ready."

"You know what? I don't think Mindy's printer works here. Why don't you run home and get that email. Print it out and bring it back."

"OK Mom." Happy to be doing something, anything, James quickly left the house and raced the short distance down Pruitt Lane.

# CHAPTER SEVENTEEN

"Dad I don't know if I can stand another night in here."

Nightfall found them still adrift in the raft. The endless monotony of sea, sky and fog had created a new level of melancholy and despair. The time since they had shot the last flare had been spent in silence. The occasional shift of a body was the only movement inside. Outside, the wind and seas rocked and jolted the craft ceaselessly; inside the crew was lifeless even though they kept hearing the distant hum of engines.

Mitchell and Calista kept vigil over their father, but they had given up on trying to keep him awake. Whenever one discovered him sleeping they would shake him gently until they got a reaction, and then leave him alone.

Calista repeated, "Dad, I don't know if I can do another night in here."

This time, the comment that came from his little girl got his attention.

"You'll be fine Calista. They're looking for us now. They'll find us."

"I don't know Dad. I wished I told Mom I love her before we left."

"Don't worry Sweetheart; your Mom knows that you love her."

"Yeah, but I can't remember the last time I told her."

"It was probably the day before we left honey. You tell her all the time."

"But I can't remember." She said plaintively.

Dale let it go and silence once again reigned over the tiny space; its occupants were alone with their thoughts. Calista thought about the amazing coincidence of her talk with Cousin Shelby in the kitchen before the trip.

*Has your dad ever wrecked a boat?*

*No, Shelby.........Jeez! Better knock on wood huh? Knock, knock, knock.*

Silently, Calista cried. For some foolish reason, she didn't want the others to know she was crying. But her heart and fear overcame her. She put her hands together and prayed silently.

*God, why? Why is this happening? I don't understand. I can't take this much longer. I don't want to do it anymore. God, I have a request that I want you to grant me. I think I've earned it after all. Well, maybe I haven't. I know I've been swearing a lot out here and I'm sorry for that. But everything that's happened since that stupid boat sank; I think I've earned this one simple request.*

*Here it is God. If you're going to take me, do it now. Do it tonight. PLEASE GOD! If you're going to let me live then that's fine, but if I'm going to die please make it happen tonight. Just do it while I'm sleeping please. I'm tired and I'm going to sleep now, but I just wanted to make that request. By the way, if I do die tonight, please make sure that my Mom and Grandma know that I love them and that I'm sorry I didn't tell them that before I left on this stupid trip.*

When Calista finished her prayer she was crying. She wept silently until she fell asleep for what would be her third and final night aboard the tiny life raft.

When James returned with the printed photo of the drifting seine in his hand, he whipped straight through the crowd to one of the few males in the house. Steve Russell was standing next to a map of Kodiak that someone had pinned to the wall. It was a nautical map of the island including Shelikof Strait. He was marking their last known location in pencil on the map.

"Steve, it's his."

"Are you sure?" Steve replied while taking a seat at the table.

"Pretty sure, you know. We went and picked the thing up at the dock last Saturday. I'm sure it's the one."

Steve was sick at heart at the news. He believed that if Dale's seine was found near their last known location it was likely that the *Magnum* had sunk there. What was even worse was that they had been out there a long time. Steve had been doing the math in his head. Dale had called Mindy at 10:00 P.M. on Wednesday and 48 hours later, they discovered the seine in the same area. Steve had been around the salmon fishing business enough to know that successful rescues usually occur soon after a disaster takes place. Not many Alaskan stories tell of crews lasting long periods of time on the water. There's just too much open space, cold weather, and stormy seas.

*That's a hell of long time to be out there.*

Steve quickly stifled his feelings of despair when he learned that the seine was Dale's. He realized that he was surrounded by several women who were looking to him for strength. His reaction would mean a great deal and, partly because of the demand for positive vibes only, he chose to keep it on that level.

"The first thing you need to do, Robinette, is call The Commander and tell him that the net is Dale's."

The news traveled quickly throughout the house that Dale's net had been found. Some cried. Others quickly walked out the front door, dialing cell phones along the way. A strange, anxious murmur reverberated through the crowd.

"You got it Steve." Robinette replied matter-of-factly as she picked up the phone.

Steve returned to the map on the wall and darkened an X on the approximate spot where the net was found. Someone crying in the other room could be heard sobbing, "Oh my God, the boat went down." Mindy looked at Steve.

"He could have dumped the net." Steve said in a level tone. He knew the room needed something positive to hear.

"Why would he do that?"

"He got into trouble and dumped the thing to save weight or get to the lazarette hatch. I don't know how heavy he was, but weight could have been a problem."

Robinette hung up the phone, ending the call with the Commander.

"That's exactly what he said. He called it a 'data point'. I guess it's a starting place for the search. He said it's a good thing. It's a good thing Mindy."

Suddenly, Mindy grabbed Felicia's arm and whisked her out of the dining room, through the living room, into the half-bathroom off of the living room. Together inside the small restroom, Mindy closed the door and locked it. Then she sat on the closed toilet seat, put her head in her hands and had her second total meltdown.

"Felicia, there's too many people out there," she muttered while gesturing toward the door. "I love them, but there's just too many."

Mindy had been valiant so far, but Felicia could feel that she was nearing another ground zero so she decided to take action. She counseled and helped Mindy get herself together before they exited the bathroom together. Tanya was waiting outside when they came out. Felicia asked her to take Mindy upstairs to her room for a break. Tanya obliged and took Mindy's hand and led her upstairs.

Felicia then found Robinette in the crowded room.

"Rob, she's starting to lose it I think. We need to clear this house. Criers and the partiers have to go. Help me get their attention will you?" Robinette raised her voice to full volume.

"HEY! Everybody listen up! Quiet! Listen! Please!" The crowd of well-wishers quieted and Robinette turned to her friend and gave her a go ahead nod. Felicia stood up on one of the dining room chairs.

"Hey everybody. We………Mindy really appreciates all the support during this, but this is getting out of hand. Without being too rude, some of you have to leave. Mindy doesn't need any extra crying in this house. She's holding up most of the time and so we need to support her. This is a search and rescue, not a wake. We need to close down. It's after ten now. At this point it'd be best if people let Mindy know they're here for her and go home and wait for news. Mindy knows you're here for her, but you can't just hang around here all night waiting for news. We can't have that."

The crowd milled about a bit but most people left eventually. Felicia asked her friend, Karen Lambert, to monitor the front door. Karen is an attorney in town and she cleared out the place in a hurry. She would make sure any new arrivals were instructed in the new house rules.

Meanwhile, Felicia grabbed Robinette, Rhoda, and Susie and said, "Come on, let's pray."

They ran upstairs to find Tanya and Mindy giggling. They were lying on the bed together and talking about all the ways they'd be *putting a hurt on Dale* when he got home.  The six women laughed together like sisters for a short while.  It relieved some of the tension for a short while.  But quickly their chatter died out.  Silence fell.

"Come on girls, let's pray," Mindy finally whispered.

The six friends stood up next to the bed and joined hands in a circle.  Again they put Mindy in the middle, bowed their heads and listened to Felicia deliver another inspirational invocation.

"I'm going back downstairs," Mindy declared after Felicia's prayer and walked out the door.  "Time for another call to the Coast Guard, Robinette; let's find out what's going on."

It was midnight.  Most of the people had taken the hint and cleared out.  The atmosphere was much less chaotic since they had laid down the ground rules to the remaining supporters.

Just then, the phone rang.  The *Phone warden* picked it up after one ring.

"Pruitt residence."

"Robin, this is Todd."

"Hi Todd, what' ya got for me?"  Robinette looked around to notice that all eyes were on her.

"Unfortunately Robin, we have to shut down the search for the night."

"Todd, don't tell me this. We can't hear this." She gestured at the anxious crowd as if to indicate that the news was bad, but not the ultimate bad news. This brought some relief to the anxious guests.

"Robin my flight crew has maxed out on their hours. I can't put them in danger, and I can't have another crew ready until first light. I do want you to know that, to a person, they all wanted to continue flying. Unfortunately, that can't happen."

"What happens tomorrow then?"

"We have the Spar en route right now to the scene. At first light, we'll send two Jayhawks and a Dolphin out. We've sent everything we have after Dale and the kids. We'll be back at it at first light, Robin."

"Well I guess that's going to have to do then. Thank you Todd, we really appreciate your work and pass our thanks on to any of the crews if you get a chance. Let them know we're grateful."

"Will do, Robin. Now remember you have my cell number. I'm going home now, but you can call me at any time for any reason. I'll be back to the office at around five A.M., but don't let that stop you from calling me. I'm here for you. Tell Mindy to hang in there."

"I will Todd. You're wonderful. Thank you."

Robinette hung up the phone and relayed the news to those who were still around.

"So I guess this means it's time to get ready for bed huh?" Susie yawned. "Let's hit the hay".

Silently, Tanya went out on the balcony to call her husband Travis. The cold air gave her chills. She feared she was losing it.

"Travis, they called off the search."

"I know. I heard. How are you holding up?"

"I'm not holding up! I can't do this anymore. I have to come home." Normally she'd have felt tremendous guilt at saying such a thing, but in this moment of weakness she couldn't hold back.

"They're gone Travis." Silence followed the words as they hung in the cold, dark Alaskan night. "They're gone and I can't go back in there and lie to my friend anymore." She was crying.

"You have to go back in there, Tanya. It's what you have to do. She needs you. It's not over yet, honey. Your friend needs you." Tanya knew he was right. Summoning up all her courage after calling her husband, she went back in the house to get ready for bed.

The remaining stragglers were giving Mindy hugs and words of encouragement as they filed out of the Pruitt home. Soon the only ones left were Susie, Tanya, Robinette, Felicia, and Lisa Johnson. As if it were old hat, Mindy and Tanya went off to bed. They slept in Dale and Mindy's room. The rest of the team sat for a few minutes decompressing and figuring out sleeping arrangements. Felicia decided that she needed to go home since her house was full of Mitchell and Calista's friends. She also had to help her son get off on his fishing trip in the morning. Robinette and Susie decided to sleep in Mitchell's bed upstairs and Lisa Johnson took the couch.

Lying upstairs in Mitchell's bed, Susie and Robinette talked *what ifs*. It was the one time that they allowed themselves to entertain the thought that Dale and the kids weren't going to make it. They didn't like it, but they could not suppress these dark thoughts completely. It was natural to voice their fears out of Mindy's hearing, but they ended that topic of conversation quickly.

Susie made one quiet call to her husband who was still out fishing in Bristol Bay. He stated the obvious, that it was cold. Of course, the women logically knew this to be true, but hearing it from one who was out on the water brought the reality of the situation even closer.

At two A.M., the last thing that was said before the two friends drifted off to sleep was, "tomorrow's going to have to be the day."

# CHAPTER EIGHTEEN

Calista opened her eyes to see that the sun was up. "I'm still here," she whispered to herself. She remembered her prayer from the night before. She was still alive! Calista felt a joy that she hadn't felt since the day she left her home on this voyage. She knew they'd be rescued today. Today was the day. She just knew it.

She heard something as well; a new sound. In her sleepy state it took her a few moments to realize what it was. It was coming from the outside, but it wasn't a boat or plane. The sound was steady, unchanging. Rain!

She quickly moved toward the flap; waking Cally and Mitchell in the process. Flinging the flap open she put out a hand and confirmed.

It was raining! The rain was moderate and steady; much more than the drizzle that had teased them yesterday.

"Dad! It's raining!" She screamed, not necessarily to the delight of her brother.

"Calista, shut up," her brother replied reflexively.

Dale stirred from his sleep at the news.

"You sure?"

"Uh, I think I'd know if it were raining." She couldn't resist sarcasm even in the most trying of times.

Dale stuck his head from beneath the canopy to confirm the news. Sure enough, it was raining. Snapping awake, they went to work on the interior water catch.

An hour's worth of working the spigot produced a good sized cup of fresh rainwater for each crew member. Nothing had ever tasted better than the feeling of that pure, cool water trickling down the back of their parched throats.

It was Saturday morning. They had already spent more than 58 hours in the confined quarters of the raft. Each crew member knew they couldn't last much longer. But the water lifted their spirits, renewed their energy, and gave them hope.

"We could last a couple more days now."

The crew scowled at the skipper. His words hung in the rank, damp air of the tight quarters. They lingered until Mitchell finally broke the silence.

"Dad! I can't believe you said that!" This led to a short burst of nervous laughter; followed by more silence. The day before, the crew's mood had fluctuated wildly. Brief moments of bonding, laughter, joy, and singing always died out quickly. Time had been dominated by what seemed to be mammoth stretches of silence; time spent alone with nothing but their own thoughts.

Now again, on Saturday morning, the elation of obtaining water aboard the life raft had been beaten down by more false alarms. Again, they thought they had heard engines. Much quarreling took place as the crew debated whether or not they heard anything at all. Initially one of the kids would climb over to the flap and look around, but now they didn't bother. A state of dread was beginning to take over.

More time passed. Boredom was the prevailing norm. The crew was getting desperate. Physically, they were better because of having had some water. But emotionally they had begun to lose hope.

Despite suffering from major hypothermia, Dale felt confident that they would be found. He knew that there would be a full-scale search on for them now. He felt bad about everything, but knew that they'd be found.

His young crew had been heroic, but they were his constant worry. He had long since given up counseling them about the emotional issues of this ordeal. The kids were merely trying to hang on, and so was he.

Calista, Mitchell, and Cally had taken shifts looking after Dale. They tried to make sure that someone was always awake with him. Mostly they tried to keep him awake, but 62 hours on the open sea is a long time. In the moments that he did sleep aboard that life raft, one of the crew usually watched to make sure he was breathing.

But now, having been refreshed with water, the entire crew of the *F/V Magnum* slept soundly aboard the tiny life raft. It was approximately 8:00 on Saturday morning, June 23rd.

The small, modern fishing village of Kodiak, Alaska woke up buzzing. Coast Guard pilots and crews readied their crafts. Small planes were prepped as friends of Dale and Mindy organized private searches. Phones had been ringing off the hook since first light. One of those calls had been between Commander Trippert and Robinette.

"Good morning Todd."

"Good morning Robin. How is Mindy doing this morning?"

"Mindy is a machine. She made coffee and is acting like a hostess to any visitors coming around. She's pretty strong. We're keeping it real positive over here Todd."

"That's good Robin. We'll do everything we can today to find Dale and those kids. We have two helicopters in the air as we speak and the Spar is currently on the scene searching the coastline." This came as no surprise to those in the house that morning since they had been hearing planes and helicopters flying overhead since about 5:15 A.M.

Robinette, Susie, Lisa, Mindy and Tanya had started the day with a prayer circle upstairs in the bedroom. All the women's prayers had taken place in Mindy's room. They hadn't felt comfortable praying downstairs in the midst of all those people. So they prayed upstairs.

This morning wouldn't be the same however. During the ordeal Felicia had been the spiritual leader. She had led all of the prayer circles. Something about the way she prayed gave Mindy inner peace and strength in the face of these terrible circumstances. But Felicia was at home with her kids, so Robinette led the morning's prayer.

As she was preparing to speak, her mind wandered, then focused. Recently, at work Robinette had been listening to a Christian radio program. She hadn't been sure what had drawn her to this program. Previously she hadn't listened to religious music on the radio. But something had drawn her to this program and she had become a daily listener for almost six months. She had particularly liked a song called *Sight Beyond What I See*, by Yolanda Adams. She knew the words by heart. As a matter of fact, she couldn't get this song out of her head during this entire ordeal. Now, as she prepared to lead the morning's prayer circle without Felicia, Robinette felt warmth in her heart. She had the feeling God had been preparing her for this moment. They joined hands in a circle around their friend. She began to pray.

With strength, courage, and hope Mindy Pruitt walked downstairs to see that the house was already starting to fill up with well-wishers.

Felicia had forgotten her towel. She stood dripping in the shower with no towel. Carefully, she stepped out and peeked around the corner to see scads of teenagers asleep in her house. She decided she had to go for it. She dashed to the towel closet, grabbed one and covered up, undetected.

She wanted to get back to the house to be with Mindy, but Paul had to get his gear for the trip and she needed to help him with that. She woke him up and told him to get ready.

"Have they found them yet?" He asked.

"No, not yet, honey." She had already called Robinette to check on things. Robinette told her about her talk with Commander Trippert that morning.

She also told Felicia that Mindy was asking about her.

"She wants you here Felicia. I led the prayer this morning, but we need you back."

"Really?" The news made her feel good.

"Yeah, I thought I gave a fine prayer, but she wants you back," Robinette replied sarcastically.

"Hah, that's funny Rob. I have to get Paul squared away and then I'll get over there just as soon as I can."

"OK Felicia, I'm going to run home for a shower, too. I'll see you back here at the house."

Felicia and her son left the house and headed down Mill Bay Road toward the harbor.

# Chapter Nineteen

The National Oceanic and Atmospheric Administration (NOAA) was formed in 1970. A compilation of several other United States agencies, NOAA consisted of the United States Coast and Geodesic Survey, the Weather Bureau, and the Bureau of Commercial Fisheries. NOAA is presently an agency of the United States Department of Commerce.

During 2007, NOAA conducted a bottom trawl survey in the Gulf of Alaska. The goals of the survey were to analyze the distribution, relative size, composition, and biological characteristics of the bottom fish in the area.

They calculated the catch per unit effort for more than 20 species of bottom fish in the Gulf of Alaska. This expedition was the fifth biennial survey of bottom fish in this area.

The three fishing vessels involved in the expedition were the *F/V Gladiator, F/V Vesteraalen,* and *F/V Sea Storm.* On Friday, each ship had heard the Coast Guard PAN PAN and knew that the *F/ V Magnum* was long overdue.

Early Saturday morning, the *Sea Storm* was steaming approximately ten knots per hour along the southwestern edge of Kodiak Island. NOAA scientists were on-deck preparing for their next survey task, while Captain Steve Branstiter and his engineer, Dan were talking in the wheelhouse. The ship's auto-pilot did most of the navigating.

"Hey Steve, what do you suppose that is out there?" The deep drawl of the engineer filled the cabin as he changed the subject and pointed out toward the water up ahead.

"Not sure," replied Steve. He slid off of his tall Captain's chair and stood up closer to the window pane to get a better look. As they drew closer he was able to make out a blue five-gallon bucket floating by. "I think it's a bucket."

"I bet that thing's off that boat, *The Magnum.*"

"It very well could be," replied the skipper.

"We oughta keep our eye out."

"Yeah, I suppose so."

The relationship between the Coast Guard and the local commercial fishing fleet has often been strained. To the owner-operators of small Alaskan family fishing businesses, the Coast Guard tends to represent costly governmental regulation and strict rules that make their jobs more difficult.

However, commercial fishing in Alaska is a dangerous lifestyle. When a fisherman is truly up against it, the Coast Guard is his best friend.

In rescue operations of this kind, searchers try to establish a search grid based on a data point. The data point in this case was the location of the *Magnum's* seine that was found floating in the Shelikof Strait near Jute Bay. Planes and helicopters systematically traversed the grid in order to avoid searching the same place over and over.

Some fishermen back home in Kodiak wondered about Coast Guard strategy in this case. The seine hadn't moved, which in all likelihood meant that it was still attached to the Magnum below. If Dale had dropped his seine to lose weight or access the lazarette, the net would be drifting with the winds and currents.

Back at the Pruitt house, Steve Russell figured one of three things had probably happened. The crew had either made it to shore in the skiff, they had drifted into the middle of the Shelikof Strait in a life raft, or they were dead.

He carefully chose not to share this last scenario with the others in the room. But as more and more time passed, Steve felt the odds of finding them alive was diminishing rapidly.

Meanwhile, out in the waters of the Shelikof Strait, the Coast Guard tirelessly continued to search. Search and rescue personnel had pleaded with their commanders to let them keep looking the previous night. Unfortunately, protocol required that the weary crew come in for rest. On Saturday morning however, an all-out search for the crew of the *F/V Magnum* had ramped up again.

Mindy was on the phone leaving another message on Calista's cell when Felicia returned. The house was packed with friends. Mindy immediately made her way to Felicia and held her in a warm embrace.

"We need to pray."

Felicia looked around the room. Some guests were drinking Baileys and coffee. A couple had Budweisers in their hands. Not exactly a praying crowd at ten in the morning she thought. Mindy began to lead her upstairs to their prayer spot when Felicia held back.

"No Mindy. We're going to do it right here."

Felicia noticed that all eyes were on them so she addressed the crowd.

"Listen up everybody! We're going to say a prayer right here in this place," pointing down at the hard-wood floor of the main room of the house as she said it. "We've been going upstairs to pray, but we're not doing that anymore. We're going to do it in this spot so anybody who wants to join in the circle is welcome and anyone who doesn't, that's fine too. I just ask that you respect our time by being quiet or stepping outside for a few minutes."

Felicia expected that many would join the prayer circle when she said it, but figured that a large group would sit it out.

What happened next surprised her.

Every man, woman, and child in the Pruitt house that morning slowly moved to form a large circle. Some set down drinks to solemnly join in.

Felicia led the group in an inspiring prayer that brought most to tears. Many felt close to God at this moment. Some had scarcely been to church, but all felt a connection to hope building in their hearts.

She then retold a parable in which a hungry man knocks on his neighbor's door and asks for bread. When he gets no answer he keeps knocking. Finally, he knocks on the door until his neighbor relents and gives him some food.

*We're not going away Lord. We're not leaving. We're going to keep knocking until we get what we need. It's what you've taught us, and it's what we're going to do.*

When Felicia finished, people moved about the room exchanging hugs, shedding tears, and offering words of hope and encouragement.

Just then Rhoda felt her cell phone vibrating. She went outside to the deck to take the call.

# CHAPTER TWENTY

The weary crew of the *F/V Magnum* was asleep when they first heard the unmistakable sound. An approaching vessel's twin diesels quickly became louder and louder. The survivors quickly began to wake up.

"Dad do you hear something?" The sentence had been repeated so many times that Dale didn't even respond...........at first.

"What is that?"

Sixty-two hours adrift had made them leery of their own senses. Their hopes had been raised and dashed again and again. Fearing to believe their ears, they played it cool for a moment.

But this was different. This time they heard voices. All four crew members were certain that something was out there.

"Mitchell, open the flap."

Mitchell scooted to his knees and opened the flap to the most glorious sight he had ever beheld.

"Dad, you're not gonna believe this! We're outta here!"

The young man had graduated from high school less than a month ago. He had felt such happiness on that night, but that was nothing compared to the feelings he had when he saw the NOAA vessel. This moment trumped that night a thousand times. This was unlike anything he had ever felt. The smile on his face betrayed the pure joy and relief in his heart. He would never forget this moment.

Approaching the raft from a distance of about fifty yards was a fishing vessel. They were saved! Cally, Calista, Mitchell and Dale yelled and screamed and hugged and cried. And they all jostled each other to get a peek at the boat. Eventually, all four wiggled their way to the flap and looked out together. It was the most beautiful ship they had ever seen! The huge grins on their faces confirmed it.

As the *Sea Storm* scaled back its engines, the crew of the *F/V Magnum* waved at them. Several crew members of the rescuing vessel stood at the rail and waved back as they approached.

The Pruitts were now positive that they had been seen. They had been seen. They were being rescued.

The realization that they were going to make it home left them limp with relief.

"You guys off the *Magnum*?" Captain Steve called out to them.

"Yeah that's us!" Dale yelled back.

The leased vessel, *F/V Seastorm* gently pulled alongside the tiny life raft. A large black and white sign amidships read, NOAA RESEARCH. Mitchell glanced at the sign as he steadied himself at the open end and prepared to dock. A *Seastorm* crewmember tossed a line that sailed over Mitchell's outstretched arms and slapped into the sea behind them. Cally immediately panicked.

"Oh my God, Mitchell! Go get it!"

"Cally! Chill! They're not going to leave us here just because they missed on the first throw."

The *Sea Storm* throttled back its diesels. Cally calmed down when she saw the deck hand about to throw another time. The second try landed right in Mitchell's arms. All his muscles tensed as the *Sea Storm's* crew pulled them snug against the steel hull. Mitchell secured the line to a strap on the side of the life raft.

Each crewmember of the Magnum gave a final horrified look at the inside of their sea-going 62 hours prison. The tiny raft was dwarfed by the 120 foot trawler as Calista, Dale, Cally and Mitchell Pruitt took turns climbing the ladder to the haven of the *Sea Storm*.

Calista reached the rail of the boat with the assistance of several crew members. She climbed over and onto the deck of the NOAA vessel.

"Sorry I smell bad," Calista joked.

The crew laughed, reassuring her that it was OK. Calista noticed immediately that there were female crewmembers. She was happy about this. Women aboard fishing vessels in Alaska can be a rarity, but this was great news since she would need some help getting out of her stinky survival suit. Sixty-two hours trapped in a survival suit is not very hygienic. The two girls felt relieved that women were there to help them.

The next person to climb aboard the *Sea Storm* was Captain Dale Pruitt. He was giddy with excitement. He ran around on the deck of the NOAA vessel like a ten-year old boy on Christmas morning. The crew of the Sea Storm was amused at his exuberance. He finally began to realize that the 62 hour ordeal was over and they were all safe. Captain Steve Branstiter assured him that he could call his wife soon. He also encouraged Dale to come inside and get warm.

"You must be freezing. Let's get all of you taken care of first, Dale. I need to call the Coast Guard and let them know the situation."

He went into the wheelhouse and began calling the Kodiak Air Station on the VHF radio. After Dale saw that his crew was being taken care of, he followed Captain Branstiter into the wheelhouse.

The skipper made several attempts to contact the Coast Guard, but couldn't get a clear connection. He finally got an answer from a nearby fishing boat. That vessel's skipper then relayed messages to the Coast Guard for him.

"The entire crew of the *F/V Magnum* is safe aboard the NOAA research vessel *Sea Storm*. All four survivors are safe and healthy. They're in good condition, but a little cold. My crew is busy getting them into dry clothes."

Dale was listening to the radio conversation from behind Captain Branstiter. Long breaks divided each transmission as the captain of the other fishing vessel relayed information back and forth between the *Sea Storm* and the Coast Guard.

He could hear the fisherman's voice coming over the radio.

*Will you need the Coast Guard's assistance retrieving survivors?*

Steve pressed the button and lifted the transmitter to his mouth. "No, unnecessary! All four are in fair condition. No life-threatening emergencies. We have a well-trained NOAA staff here. We will bring them in;

should be in Kodiak in approximately sixteen hours. Over"

*Roger that, Captain. Coast Guard says if you feel like their condition worsens and requires immediate medical attention let us know and they'll come get them.*

"Roger. We'll have them back soon."

The look on Dale's face reminded Captain Steve Branstiter of what they had been through. All the fear, horror, and relief were mirrored in Dale's expression.

"You ready for some clean, dry clothes Dale?" The Captain handed over small stack of clothes that his crew had rounded up.

"You all need to wait on showers. It's best to warm you up gradually and make sure you get hydrated before you take a hot shower. You can change downstairs."

"Thanks Steve," Dale said as he moved by him and headed toward the stairs that led down to the cabin, "I appreciate that."

"Let me run up the line a bit and try to get a signal on this *sat* phone here. By the time you get in those clothes and some warm hot chocolate in you, I should be able to get your wife on the line."

"Again Steve, a thank you doesn't seem like enough," Dale said as he descended the stairs with his pile of clothes.

Dale changed quickly in the stateroom below. He was still running on pure adrenaline. He felt great. He emerged from the room to see Mitchell standing in the galley, drinking hot chocolate and talking to a few *Sea Storm* crewmembers. The girls were nowhere to be seen. Wordlessly, Dale walked up to his son and gave him a huge bear hug. Mitchell reciprocated. He never wanted the hug to end. His father's huge grin would have given the sun a run for its money.

# CHAPTER
# TWENTY-ONE

"They found them!" Rhoda barely kept her voice to a whisper as she spoke to Felicia on the deck. Almost immediately, Felicia's cell buzzed. Her call came from her ex-husband. Same news.

Rhoda and Felicia were bug-eyed with excitement. They quickly embraced and frantically motioned Robinette to come out on the deck. Trying to keep their voices under control they shared the news that was coming in from the fleet of Kodiak fisherman out in nearby waters.

"Oh my God! " Robinette cupped her hands together in front of her mouth to hide her emotion at the news. "We have to get confirmation from Todd, though. Don't say anything. Mindy can't hear this until we hear it from the source. We're not going there."

Pretending nonchalance, they slipped back into the house, but they could tell that the news was already out of the bag. Felicia urged quiet. If it turned out not to be true, it would kill Mindy. She couldn't know until they had official confirmation from Todd.

Mindy was at the far end of the house at the time, so Robinette dialed Commander Todd Trippert in Juneau.

"Todd, we're hearing some stuff here. What are you hearing?"

"We're not sure Robin. Can you hang on a minute?" He put her on hold for a few moments and then returned. "We have something, but we're not sure."

"What?" With a badly concealed wobble in her voice, Robinette prodded him hard for an answer. "Talk to me Todd, talk to me. Do you have news for me? I need for you to have news for me."

There was a silence on the other end of the line that seemed to be interminable. Commander Trippert was getting information, but wanted to be absolutely sure of his facts before he spoke.

Finally: "Robin, we have confirmation that they've been rescued and are all in good health."

"YES!"

The scream came from the depths of her soul. Spontaneous shouting and applause erupted throughout the house. It was as if gold were coming out of the sky and bombs were bursting in the air. People laughed, cried, hugged and danced. Tears streamed down most faces as enormous bursts of adrenalin were released in those rooms.

Dale and the kids had been rescued and they were coming home to Pruitt Lane.

Mindy was surrounded in her home by her loved ones, her extended Kodiak family. Everyone wanted to share in this joyous occasion. For the briefest and most beautiful of moments, Mindy rejoiced. She joined in the wonderful celebration with her family and friends.

The elation was short-lived however. She was overjoyed and grateful in her response to the news of her family's rescue. But her pounding headache and fast departing energy left her drained. She still wanted more information about their condition. Mindy wanted to feel and touch her touch her family. She needed to lay hands on their actual flesh. Mindy had a great need to talk them before she could let her guard down. The relief of the moment was fierce, but she was still on defense. Mindy's defense is good; it's a survival skilled honed by years as a fisherman's wife.

Her mood began to fade. Her inner circle sensed the shift; it was time to get back to their primary work of getting more information.

"I need to talk to Dale." Mindy blurted to no one in particular. They took it to heart and began to brainstorm about how to accomplish this since they had no satellite phone.

Someone in the house suggested the easiest way to do so might be to run down to the Ocean Beauty Cannery and use the *sat* phone there.

"Great idea! Tanya, take me to the cannery. I'll use Tim's phone to call them out there."

A party was breaking out at the house. People continued to dance around and drink toasts to the rescuers and crew. Robinette was still on the phone with Commander Todd Trippert.

"Todd you are the best! You are the man. I am so happy. We're all so happy and thankful. We can't thank you enough."

Mindy was standing next to Robinette as she tried to listen to the conversation over the din in the house. "Let me talk to him," she implored Robinette.

"Listen Todd, it's a little hard to hear you over all the noise in this place. Mindy wants to talk to you. I'm going to quiet this place down so you two can talk."

Through the entire ordeal Mindy had yet to speak to Commander Trippert. Robinette had played the role of communications specialist in the house (Mindy's preference). Now she wanted to give her own thanks to the Coast Guard.

The noisy crowd continued to grow and Robinette made an effort to quiet them.

"Hey! Listen up! Mindy's talking to the CG. Quiet down for minute will you." The command drew the noise level down slightly.

"Hi, Commander Trippert."

"Hello Mrs. Pruitt. Congratulations. I'm very happy for you."

"Well there's just nothing I could possibly say that could express my gratitude to you and your crew. You were so helpful and professional with us. I'm just very, very happy and I thank you...." Her voice trailed off.

"Mrs. Pruitt this is what we're here for and we're just happy that they've been found and that they're healthy. The skipper of the *Sea Storm* reported to us that they're cold and hungry, but in excellent spirits."

"Oh my God, thank you."

"It's our pleasure Mrs. Pruitt. I just informed Robin that the *Sea Storm* has offered to bring them on into port for us. We don't like to hoist people up in the baskets unless absolutely necessary, so this will be the safest and most comfortable way to proceed. They should be in to port in approximately sixteen hours."

"Thank you. Thank you so much Commander. Your people are the greatest." Mindy noticed Robinette looking over her shoulder.

"Don't hang up," she whispered to her, "I want to talk to him again."

"Hey listen Commander Trippert, Robinette is bugging me to let her talk to you again so thank you, thank you, thank you again. I am so grateful to you and your crew. Thank you."

"You're welcome and you take care of that family of yours when they return." The words spread warmth and joy to Mindy's heart. She handed the receiver to Robinette.

"Hi, Todd. I just want to let you know that you are the best. Something I didn't tell you through this whole ordeal is that I NEVER let anyone call me Robin."

"Oh, I'm sorry Robinette."

"Oh no sir, that's not what I meant. I want you to know that you can call me Robin any time. You are a true American hero. I'll never forget you."

"Well that makes me feel great to hear you say, Robin. The Pruitts must be a special family judging by the reaction to all of this. They have some wonderful friends."

"Well you're right they ARE a special bunch. And thanks to you, they're coming home!" She was practically screaming into the phone. "Todd, I have to let you go. Mindy is getting ready to go to the cannery to talk to Dale and I want to say goodbye to her."

"OK, then Robin. Nicely done over there. You take care and feel free to call anytime for anything."

"Thanks Todd. You take care now. Goodbye."

Exuberant well-wishers lined the road and waved at the Chevy as Tanya pulled away from the house. The crunch of gravel under-wheel on Pruitt Lane was drowned by the hoots and hollers of relieved and happy well-wishers.

Inside the truck, Tanya and Mindy politely waved back, but soon fell into silence. Euphoria had given way to exhaustion. The normally chatty friends became less talkative as they drove toward the cannery.

Mindy called Tim Blott en route to make sure that he was ready and that contact could be made with the *Sea Storm.*

He assured her that everything was a go. Initially, communication signals had been spotty between the *Sea Storm* and the Coast Guard. But Tim informed Mindy that the signal was good.

"Hi Mindy."

"Oh my God, Dale." Spontaneous tears streamed down at the sound of his voice. Tanya stood by her friend's side as she talked in the office of the Ocean Beauty cannery.

"I guess you heard that we've been rescued."

"Yeah we heard. How are you?"

"We're fine, Mindy. We're aboard the *Sea Storm* and we're all fine."

"What about Calista? Are you sure they shouldn't medivac her in here?"

"No, I don't think that'll be necessary. She's down below with Cally now with a couple of the female crew members here. They're NOAA people Hun; real professional crew. They know what they're doing and everyone agrees that we'll be fine coming in with them."

"I'm so glad you're safe Dale, this has been hell."

"I know it has sweetheart. I just feel real bad that I put you through this. I'm sorry."

"Oh geez Dale. I got other people here listening so don't you get too mushy," she said laughing as she wiped the tears from her eyes. "You keep warm and get some rest on the way in. We'll be looking out for you in a bit honey."

"OK Mindy. You get some rest too. I love you."

"I love you too. Hug those kids for me."

Dale reached above his head and returned the hand-held receiver to its cradle. Sitting in the wheelhouse of the *Sea Storm* he looked out into the thick fog that enshrouded them. Visibility was poor. He realized just how lucky they were. Had the *Sea Storm* been perhaps 50 yards in either direction they surely wouldn't have been seen. They'd still be in the raft. They had been onboard the NOAA boat for less than an hour and their ordeal was fading. It seemed as though it had been a terrible dream.

Crew members aboard the *Sea Storm* were busy securing the life raft on the deck. They used the ship's crane to hoist the raft from the ocean below to the aft deck of the vessel. In the wheelhouse, Steve set a course to Kodiak. Dale, Cally, Calista, and Mitchell were warm and dry, and looking forward to eating a good meal.

They were damned happy to be there in a warm dry place; no matter what the circumstances were.

Exuberance was the dominant mood aboard the NOAA research vessel that day. A mere half-hour before, things had been pretty routine on the *Sea Storm*. Crews aboard working vessels in and around Kodiak fluctuate effortlessly between mundane passing of time and bouts of heavy labor. Before they found the Magnum, this crew had been mostly killing time on their way to their next research task. Now, they hustled about the small ship tending to their surprise passengers' every need. They went all out to make them comfortable. The survivors were very grateful for their kindness.

"Mitchell you want a cappuccino?" the ship's cook asked. Mitchell was sitting upright on the padded bench at the galley table, swaddled in a blanket. Underneath the blanket, he wore dry clothes that crewmembers had rustled up for him. He felt great.

Smiling, he replied, "Can't say that I've ever had a cappuccino. What the hell is it?"

"Oh, you'll like it. I'll make you one and you can try it. You don't have to drink it if you don't like it."

Minutes later, Mitchell was enjoying his first ever cappuccino. It was like a little taste of heaven. He cupped the warm mug with both hands and looked around the cabin.

Calista and Cally emerged from a stateroom with their new found friends. They had been outfitted with cotton sweatpants, sweatshirts and dry socks. The group of women was all smiles and chatter. The crew of the *Magnum* settled in for the deadhead back to Kodiak. Delectable scents began to overpower the diesel and fish smell in the cabin as the cook prepared a feast for their guests.

The scene felt surreal for both the rescuers and the rescued. The *Sea Storm* crew mirrored fascination and disbelief as Mitchell, Dale, Calista, and Cally shared their survival story. The raft looked tiny resting on the aft deck. As the story unfolded, it was hard for them to imagine; sixty-two hours in there?

Cally shared the most. Although exhausted and pale, her lively, bright eyes riveted her listeners. She talked nearly nonstop for much of the journey back home. She told of her horror when she was jarred awake by Calista's yelling at her to put on her survival suit. She described falling out the *Magnum's* cabin door; striking her head against the steel deck-winch outside as she was falling overboard. She shared her intense fear, pain, and anguish when she found herself in the pitching, frigid sea.

The *Sea Storm's* crew sat in rapt fascination as she described wanting to give up while drifting alone. She had been ready to let go of her life in the icy waters of Alaska; but because of truly brave and courageous deeds that took place, she had survived. Cally Rose Pruitt would certainly have died that night if her cousin had not gone to her and helped her back to the raft.

Mitchell, Dale, and Calista chimed in on some parts of the story from time to time. But Cally Rose was the *big talker*. She was euphoric that she was alive....that they were all alive. She couldn't believe their good luck and it showed.

They were all surprised. But alive they were. Soon they were preparing to eat for the first time in nearly three full days. What a beautiful thing it was.

The *Sea Storm* continued chugging its way along the west coast of Kodiak Island; toward Kodiak Town. In the wheelhouse, Captains Pruitt and Branstiter chatted idly. They also passed long periods of time in wordless contemplation. During these times, Dale stared out the windows at the changing scenery. Periodically, he could see the uneven coastline of the island through the low clouds and fog. He recognized every landmark. The inlets, capes, and bays of the west coast were his backyard. At any point during the journey Dale knew he could jump off the boat, swim to shore, and hike over-land to the other side of the island; to his home but his taste for cold water swimming seemed to have left him for the moment. Home had seemed so far away during his family's predicament. Now it was so close.

Dale was still very upset with himself about the feel-ings of helplessness that had come over him in the raft. He had been in control of most everything his whole life. But he finally conceded to himself that control is fleeting when the sea is on a rampage. He had been completely helpless in the raft. The feeling had terri-fied him.

Even in the thirty to forty minutes that passed between abandoning ship and entering the life raft he had some level of control. He managed to jump from the rolling skiff to the hull of the Magnum. He fought with everything he had to pop the raft open. Clumsily, he and his crew had worked as a team to hoist them-selves, hypothermic and exhausted, from the water into the raft. But he had still maintained some level of con-trol over the situation. He and Mitchell used strength, courage, and pure will to open that raft and get the family out of the icy waters. But from the moment that they flopped into the raft, they had been at the mercy of the sea. Several pounds of rubber stitched together at the seams had been the difference between life and death. But the raft had held and kept his family alive. He found it hard to believe that the tiny vessel on the stern of the *Sea Storm* had held. It had stayed afloat and upright in high seas and they were alive to tell about it. He found it hard to believe. The sea had taught him a lesson he never wanted to forget.

Seafaring men are kept sharp by stories of tragedy and survival on the water. Some of the stories are true, some grow larger with the telling, and some are pure fiction. But the stories Dale had heard over the years had, in some way, prepared him for his own accident. He knew he had made mistakes. But he also figured that once it was certain that the *Magnum* was going down, he had mostly made all the right moves. Dale knew of great feats of strength and daring done by Kodiak men under terrible circumstances at sea. Some had lived; some had died, but all had elements of heroism. Dale had felt for some time when his time came, he would go down fighting. This had almost been his time, but Dale had lived and so had his family. Dale was heading home as a live hero. He would gladly have fought the sea to the death to save his family. But his story had a happy ending. He had saved the lives of his children; and his own life as well.

Some fishermen spend their careers in fear of being lost at sea. Others, like Dale, seem to ignore the danger.

Yet, for many quiet hours alone at the helm of the *Calista Marie* over the years, Dale felt he had been in training for what had just happened. An intense survival instinct had taken over the moment he dropped the radio and escaped the submerging wheelhouse of the *Magnum*. The quick decision to make a run for shore in the skiff had been foiled by his own precaution, the safety line. Instantly, the plan changed to jump to the hull and hope for a quick rescue. But that plan too had been overtaken by the large wave that swept Calista and Mitchell into the water. Life or death decisions made in an instant can stand out and hang around forever in the mind. For Dale, standing on the turtled hull had been one of those moments. The images of Calista and Mitchell in the water below him would be frozen forever in his memory. He had replayed the scene countless times during his time aboard the life raft. Now, in the warm comfortable confines of the *Sea Storm* wheelhouse, the scene replayed itself yet again in Captain Dale Pruitt's mind until the sound of his new friend broke through the silence.

"Dale, you know as much as I do that most of these things don't end up happy. I'm just real glad that this one did."

Staring distantly through the wheelhouse window Dale replied, "Me too, Steve. Me too."

# CHAPTER TWENTY-TWO

All of Kodiak knew. It had taken less than an hour for word to spread throughout town that the Pruitts were rescued, in good condition, and on their way home. The local radio station was broadcasting the news. Out at sea, working fishermen spread the good news over their radios. At the Coast Guard base, rescue crews returned home aboard helicopters and planes for a much deserved rest. The town was abuzz with the story of their survival..

During the ordeal, when word was out that the Pruitts were past two days overdue, hope had been in short supply. Most had kept their doubts to themselves; but everyone had them. Deep down, it had been impossible to not at least entertain the thought that Cally, Calista, Mitchell, and Dale were dead. The loss of the Pruitts would have been a body blow to Kodiak.

But it was not to be. Now an excited town bustled about planning for the homecoming. Despite the elation and complete sense of relief, Mindy's head still pounded. Her headache had been banging away for three full days. She felt numb. While happy and filled with joy that her family was alive, she was emotionally and physically exhausted. Mindy was running on empty. Returning from the cannery, a long shower and change of clothes had helped, but she needed rest. The house had largely cleared out. All that remained were Tanya and Susie. The rest of the support team of friends had gone home to their own families and their beds.

Still, sleep eluded Mindy. Tanya and Susie forced her to lie down a few times, but these naps never lasted. Something always came up that Mindy felt needed to be taken care of. Adrenaline and joy overcame pain and fatigue as she plodded her way through the day. Her family was coming home. There were people to call; plans to be made. The boat would be arriving soon. People wanted to be with them. There was going to be a homecoming on the dock at the Ocean Beauty Cannery. It was going to be a wonderful thing.

Meanwhile, on-board the *Sea Storm*, the bond developing between the two crews was remarkable. A once in a lifetime event had taken place. The voyage home allowed them some time to come terms with the enormity of it. The *Magnum* crew had looked death squarely in the eyes. Now they were casually chatting away with their new friends. Very recently they had worried about what life would be like for Mindy, Nancy, Jeff, and the rest of the family without them. In the face of grave danger they had contemplated their own deaths. And now warmly and comfortably the ladies on board sang songs from "Oh Brother Where Art Thou". Together the friends chatted as the research boat made its way back through Kupreanof Strait, through Whale Passage and the Ouzinkie Narrows. Toward *Buoy Four*, and home.

Mindy's mother and Susie embraced in front of the tiny Kodiak Airport. Susie filled Patsy in on the details of the rescue as they grabbed luggage and loaded the vehicle.

Patsy wiped tears from her eyes as they drove toward town. She had wanted to be there when Mindy received the news about her family's fate. She hadn't quite made it in time, but she lucked out. She thanked God for the beautiful news.

Having carefully eased the ship around *Buoy Four* that identifies the safest route into the Kodiak shipping channel, Captain Steve Branstiter headed for the dock. His heart was full. He knew his role in the whole saga had been purely luck. Fate perhaps. But Steve had no idea about the magnitude of the situation. An official statement with a description of the rescue and a picture of the *Sea Storm* in route to Kodiak had already been released by the Coast Guard. National media outlets like the Today Show and Oprah would soon be calling. They would be asking for pictures of the rescue. But there were none. Captain Branstiter had already polled his crew. During the excitement of the rescue, no one had taken pictures. As a testimony to the professionalism of his crew, all hands took part in securing the survivors safely on-board. None had grabbed cameras. Their first thoughts and efforts were devoted to the Pruitts.

Nonetheless, Steve wished he had a picture of those faces (especially Cally's) as they peeked from under the canopy of the life raft. It was an image of pure joy. He figured he'd never need a picture himself. The moment would always be stored in his memory bank.

*But it sure would be good to share that priceless experience with others. A picture of the four Pruitts sticking their heads out of that raft would be worth well over 1000 words.*

Just then, the Captain eased the ship through the channel toward the Fred Zharoff Bridge. The familiar graffiti message, *Don't Leave Me Babe,* was now visible high overhead above the port bow.

A lone passing fishing boat sounded a loud welcome home blast. Other boats in and around the harbor followed suit as the *Sea Storm* passed all the familiar landmarks. The ship was carrying precious cargo. That much was apparent to the NOAA crew as they approached the dock that housed the Ocean Beauty cannery; and the gathering, anxious welcome-home crowd. As Steve Branstiter eased the vessel slowly toward the pier, approximately 100 friends and family members awaited on the dock. Hoots and hollers volleyed back and forth from dock to ship. Some well-wishers were brought to tears at the sight of the Pruitts as they approached the dock aboard the *Sea Storm.*

Everyone on that dock had privately entertained the notion that the family had been lost at sea. Boats go down every year in and around Kodiak. It's not uncommon. In most cases a mayday is heard and the Coast Guard is quickly on the scene to bring survivors safely home. Often times, *Good Samaritan* rescues occur in which fellow fishermen in the fleet quickly come to the aid of a distressed crew. It is very uncommon, however, for all hands to survive sixty hours lost at sea.

Everyone involved in this saga, whether at sea or back home in Kodiak, had endured great fear and anguish. The emotional swing from that place to this had a sense of unreality. It was also awesome. An overused word perhaps, but appropriate nonetheless. A sense of awe was present as the *Sea Storm* released a long horn blast of its own on approach. The crew tossed lines over the gunwales fore and aft to eagerly awaiting deckhands from the clamoring throng on the pier. The anticipation was almost too much to bear for Calista and Cally who were anxiously scanning the crowd for their mothers.

As the crew stabilized the ship, Calista was amazed to see Grandma Patsy on the dock. She made it all the way up here from Washington State during the time they had been in the life raft. Calista also saw almost everyone else who mattered in her life. There was Shelby, Aunt Susie, Farva, James, Aunt Nancy, Uncle Jeff, Clyde, Ben, Tim and more. Calista was so thrilled to see everyone, but she wanted to hug her mom most of all. After leaving the boat, she moved into the crowd hugging her family, looking for Mindy. Finally, she saw her mother walking up toward the crowd. Calista moved toward her. They met in an enveloping embrace that she hoped would last forever.

"I love you mom." Calista was crying.

"I love you too Calista. I'm so happy that you're home. I'm so glad." Her cheeks and Calista's shone with tears.

Mitchell was immediately mauled with man hugs from his buddies as he stepped from the ship to the dock. The hugs felt great, but he eventually moved on through the crowd. He found his grandma and his girl-friend Candice and of course, his mother. Cally made her way through to her mom, Nancy and dad, Jeff. Little was said as they held each other in a warm embrace.

Dale was the last of the *Magnum* crew to leave the *Sea Storm* and step across onto the cannery pier. Dressed in dark cotton sweats, he was smiling broadly as he stepped over lines and hoses. He worked his way toward his wife.

"I'm sorry Mindy", he whispered in her ear as they hugged.

"Oh Dale." Mindy was speechless. Her head was still pounding. She was happy, but not truly jubilant. Instinctively, Mindy knew that the saga of the *Magnum* was not over. It was a joyful occasion to see her family again. She considered it the greatest of miracles. But she knew then that it wasn't over.

Mindy seemed to be in a daze as she stared at her husband. A voice from the crowd interrupted the moment.

"Hey Calista, we're going to get a picture of you four. Come on over here by the raft. Cally and Mitchell, come on over here by Dale."

Using the hydraulic crane, the *Sea Storm* crew hoisted the raft from the stern of the ship and set it gently on the dock. Mitchell, Cally, Dale, and Calista each made their way in front of the raft.

Arm in arm the four-person crew of the *F/V Magnum* posed for a picture in front of the tiny vessel. Cally tenderly rested her head on her cousin's shoulder as they posed. The four smiled gamely for the camera, but their exhaustion was apparent. The anguish and fear they had so recently endured still permeated their bodies. They were fading fast.

A voice from the crowd shouted, "I thought the whole point was to see the raft."

Calista replied punchily. "I know, I don't see the raft." The crowd laughed as a crew member grabbed the rubber raft by a handle and slid it so that half of it was visible for the cameras. The haggard bunch adjusted their line and posed again for the multiple cameras.

Cally, Mitchell, and Dale were silent as their friends, family, and rescuers clamored around them taking pictures. Cally put her head gently back onto Mitchell's shoulder. Mitchell stood stoically. The hood of his borrowed sweatshirt was up. A wry smile was sneaking out of the corner of his mouth. Dale made a second attempt to smile for the cameras, but Mindy noticed that his smile drooped at the corners. She could tell from the look in her family's eyes and in her husband's sagging smile that they had been to hell and back. They were home and she would be OK because of it. They would all be OK, eventually. But Mindy worried as her family posed in front of their life raft. Then Calista's smile returned and she said, "I don't know where to look". Again the crowd laughed.

After an hour or so of mingling, the Pruitts headed for home. Dale, Cally, Mitchell, and Calista had each hugged every person who came down to the dock that night. They felt blessed. They now belonged to a select group of people who have survived imminent death. A rare fraternity of individuals exists that have looked death in the face and lived to tell about it.

On Saturday, June 23rd of 2007 the Pruitt family drove home. Contentment filled the car, but there was no outward rejoicing. Very little conversation took place. They were four exhausted humans watching the familiar spruce forest pass by along Otmeloi Drive on the way home to Pruitt Lane. Mindy eased the vehicle to a stop in front of their house and turned off the ignition. They sat for several moments in utter silence. The stillness was balm to their battered psyches. They knew the silence would be short-lived though as friends were on their way to join in the celebration. But they soaked up the moment anyway. Slowly, they exited the car and moved toward their home and opened the door.

*Home is where your story begins.*
The Pruitts were home.

THE VIEW OF ISLAND LAKE FROM THE
BALCONY OF THE PRUITT HOME.

KODIAK SMALL BOAT HARBOR.

DOCKSIDE PHOTO SHOWS DALE STANDING IN FRONT OF THE STEAMING HOT BANYA. CALISTA, CALLY, AND MITCHELL'S SURVIVAL SUITS ARE DRAPED OVER THE RAILING. THE RAFT STILL LAYS CRUMPLED AT THE TOP OF THE STAIRS TO THE RIGHT.

Dale and Mindy Pruitt pose outside of
their home in Kodiak.

THE LEASED NOAA RESEARCH VESSEL, *SEA STORM* CHUGS HOME TO
KODIAK. THE TIRED, HAPPY CREW OF THE MAGNUM IS RESTING COM-
FORTABLY INSIDE. THE SMALL ORANGE LIFE RAFT CAN BE SEEN ON
THE STARBOARD SIDE OF THE DECK. (COURTESY OF THE USCG)

FROM LEFT: CALLY PRUITT, MITCHELL PRUITT, CALISTA PRUITT, AND DALE PRUITT. SAFE ON THE DOCK OF OCEAN BEAUTY SEAFOOD, THE CREW POSES IN FRONT OF THE RAFT THAT WAS THEIR HOME FOR NEARLY THREE DAYS. (COURTESY OF MINDY PRUITT)

15759716R00146

Made in the USA
Charleston, SC
19 November 2012